Truth, Spirituality & Contemporary Issues

Study Guide

Anne Jordan

Published in 2003 by:
Nelson Thornes Ltd
Delta Place
27 Bath Road
CHELTENHAM
GL53 7TH
United Kingdom

03 04 05 06 07 / 10 9 8 7 6 5 4 3 2 1

A catalogue record for this book is available from the British Library

ISBN 0 7487 7342 8

Edited by Nicola Haisley

Illustrations by Francis Bacon

Page make-up by Northern Phototypesetting Co. Ltd, Bolton

Printed and bound in Spain by Graphycems

Acknowledgements
With thanks to the following for permission to reproduce photographs and other copyright material in this book:

BBC, p 40; Martyn Chillmaid, p 28; Corbis, p 5; News International, p 37; Press Association, p 23, 60; Salvation Army Heritage Centre, p 59; Science Photo Library, p 15

Every effort has been made to contact copyright holders. The publishers apologise to anyone whose rights have been inadvertently overlooked, and will be happy to rectify any errors or omissions.

Contents

Introduction

This book is to help you prepare for your exam

This book is written for GCSE students studying the AQA Religious Studies Specification B, Module 4 ('Truth, spirituality and contemporary issues'). However, there are many sections that can help you revise topics appropriate to other GCSE Religious Studies courses. It is important for you to check the content of the GCSE Religious Studies examination specification for which you are entered.

In the examination you will be expected to illustrate your answer by referring to actual examples that are relevant to the question. You will also need to make use of appropriate references to religious stories, teachings and practices that you have studied.

On any moral issue, you need to make sure you know the viewpoint of **two** religious traditions. Many of the exam questions on moral issues will start by saying: 'Choose **two** different religious traditions...' This study guide has focused on Christianity only and so the religious traditions covered in this book are the major Christian traditions or **denominations**: Church of England, Catholic Church, Orthodox Church, Society of Friends (Quakers), Methodist Church. There are also points in this book when you have to compare Christianity with other religious traditions to understand how Christianity is different.

Revision tip

A **denomination** within Christianity is a church or group of Christians who have shared Christian beliefs and ways of worship.

If you have studied another religious tradition as well as Christianity in your course, you will need to revise your notes for these thoroughly.

This book looks at the key points for each topic. You will find more information in the textbook that this study guide supports, which is called *Perspectives on Religious Issues*, as well as in other textbooks. It is also a very good idea to have a copy of the exam specification for your course, which tells you what you need to have covered. Your teacher can help you with this. This book matches Unit 4 of the AQA exam board's Religious Studies Specification B GCSE.

Answering the exam questions

When you start preparing for your exam, remember that any of the examination questions set expect you to show the examiner:

- that you have knowledge and understanding of relevant teachings from sacred texts, religious leaders and organisations, and that you can evaluate these
- that you have knowledge and understanding of the different viewpoints that may exist within a religious tradition and that you can evaluate the different viewpoints
- that you have knowledge and understanding of significant secular (non-religious) responses related to the moral issues studied and you can evaluate the secular responses
- that you have knowledge and understanding of the legal position related to each of the moral issues studied and you can evaluate the legal position
- that you appreciate the relationship between religious beliefs and teachings and the way in which believers live their lives
- that you can evaluate the different viewpoints and teachings related to each issue that you have presented and that you have set out your personal response to the issue.

Remember that how well you set out your argument and how well you present it are also important in getting good marks. Try to make sure that you write clearly so the examiner can read what you are saying. Plan out your answer so it goes logically from one point to another – do not spend too long on this, just jot down a few notes to help yourself.

Read the question to make sure you have understood what it is asking and check how many marks are available for each part of the question. These tell you how important each bit of the question is and help you decide how much to write. There is not much point writing pages for a question that only gives you one or two marks. And remember, too, that you do not get marks subtracted for

Revision tip

The words used in an examination question can often be a clue as to what the examiner is looking for in your answer. The questions are examining your knowledge and understanding of the issues, as well as your ability to evaluate them. Look at the Glossary of Terms provided by the examination board you have followed as a guide to what the examiner is looking for in your answers.

wrong answers – always write something, even if your mind has gone blank. The examiner will be looking for ways to give you marks.

Each of the units in this book gives you key words you need to know. Make sure that you have learnt to spell them correctly as well as to use them accurately in your answers. There are short answer questions in the book that will help you do a quick check on how well you have understood the topic. Then at the end of the book, there are sample essay questions for you to practise your exam skills.

Keeping up to date

Your course looks at contemporary issues – 'live' issues that develop and change every day. Books like this one are useful for preparing for your exam, but they cannot provide you with up-to-date information about the topics you have studied.

You will do well in your exam, and get even more out of your course, if you try to keep up to date with contemporary issues and current affairs. Keeping up with what is in the news and making use of news items to support your answers is a very good idea.

Case studies are also a great way of making exam answers really good and they help you revise, too. A case study is an example of something that goes into a bit of detail. For example, you might use a case study of the charity Shelter to talk about religious attitudes to rich and poor in society. You could talk about the work they do, what the aims of the charity are, how they raise money, and so on. Even better than a case study, is a case study that you keep up to date! This book will give you reminders of when case studies might be useful. There are some examples, too.

You can keep up to date with contemporary issues by watching news and current affairs programmes on the television or reading articles in the newspapers. You should try to look at relevant news stories and situations and apply the beliefs and teachings of the different religious traditions to the issues. You do not have to confine yourself to news programmes, as many of the issues that you have studied are tackled in soap operas and that may help you to understand how these issues might affect people's lives.

Internet searches can provide you with material related to all the topics you have studied. The Internet will give you access to websites associated with many of the charities and organisations that you have studied. Looking on the Internet at the work of organisations will help you to revise them and keep your case studies up to date. You can also find details about the different responses of the Christian denominations to many of the contemporary issues you have studied.

If you have not got access to the Internet, you might write to many of the organisations that you have studied for information about their work. Your school or local library will be able to find the addresses of many of these organisations for you. If you do write to any organisation, remember to include a stamped addressed envelope for a reply. Most of these organisations are charities and cannot afford to pay the cost of sending you the information.

'Mum, can I watch EastEnders tonight – I need to revise for my GCSE Religious Studies exam?'

Section A

Nature and expression

The nature of truth

Revision tip

You only need to refer to **one** religious tradition in answers specifically on the nature of truth.

Revision tip

We know it is historically true that William the Conqueror invaded Britain in 1066. All historians would agree with this (or almost all). But why did he invade? Was he greedy for new land? Had the King of England promised the country to him? Different historians argue different things based upon their own interpretation of the historical evidence.

Truth is what is accepted as right and evidence is used to prove the truth. But there is more than one kind of 'truth'. The type of evidence that is used to prove something is 'true' gives us different kinds of truth. For your exam you need to know about **scientific**, **historical**, **moral** and **spiritual** truth.

Scientific truth is based upon observation, hypothesis, and experiment, including repeated testing to prove it true. Scientific truths are **objective** – they are not just one person's opinion – and so they are seen to be 'hard' truth: the most trustworthy kind. However, scientific truth is constantly changing as new results may produce new evidence that proves earlier theories untrue or inaccurate.

Historical truth is based upon documentary and archaeological evidence. Some facts about history can be backed up by very firm evidence that everyone can agree on. But historical truth about *why* things happened is **subjective** because historians each interpret this evidence for themselves. There is no proof for this kind of historical question. Different people using exactly the same evidence can have completely different views on what happened.

What people believe to be right and what they believe to be wrong is described as a **moral truth**. Moral truth is based on **abstract reasoning** – logical thinking. It is not possible to prove a moral truth by scientific experiment or historical evidence. People do not always agree about what is morally true. And the same thing can be right in some circumstances but wrong in others.

Spiritual truth is what a believer claims to be true about the existence of God, the origin of the universe, and the purpose of life. Believers do use evidence when talking about spiritual truths – there is the evidence from personal experience, abstract reasoning, and the evidence from religious teachings. But belief, trust and faith are extremely important. Believers may use evidence to reason that their beliefs are true, but the certainty that what they believe is true comes from **faith**.

In the Christian tradition, for example, religious authority is a source of spiritual truth. The Bible, especially the teachings of Jesus, the whole Christian tradition, the teachings of Christian leaders, all tell believers about the truths of Christianity. Individual Christians may also have their own religious experiences and their own abstract reasoning as sources of spiritual truth. But for all Christians, faith is much more important than looking for proof for spiritual truths.

'I cannot get an answer to my moral dilemma.'

Test yourself

1 (a) How might a scientist establish the truth of a statement?
(b) What problems are there with believing a 'scientific truth'?

2 (a) How might a historian establish the truth of a statement?
(b) What problems are there with believing a 'historical truth'?

3 (a) How do people establish 'moral truth'?
(b) What problems are there with believing a 'moral truth'?

4 (a) How do believers establish 'spiritual truth'?
(b) What problems are there with believing a 'spiritual truth'?

Claims to truth

The previous two pages looked at different kinds of truth. You also need to know about how religious traditions make claims to be true. There are three main types of these claims to truth:

- **sacred writings**
- **religious authorities**
- **conscience.**

Revision tip

You need to refer to **two** religious traditions when answering questions about claims to truth. These two pages look at differences within Christian traditions. You may have different examples to use as well as or instead of these.

Revision tip

The **fundamentalist** position looks at Biblical truth like a scientist might: it is objectively true – true for all people at all times. The **liberal** position is more like historical truth: there is plenty of evidence in the Bible, which can be interpreted in different ways.

Different religious traditions believe different things: they have different 'truths'. The different religious traditions also have different ways of expressing these truths.

In the Christian tradition, the Bible tells Christians that the truth is 'with God' and God sent the truth to earth in the form of Jesus. Jesus described himself as 'the way, the truth and the light'. After Jesus returned to heaven, Christians believe that God sent the Holy Spirit to guide people to the truth.

All Christians agree on this central message: it is the fundamental belief of Christianity. The different Christian traditions, though, do not all agree on everything. There are different views on the best way to follow God's wishes and different claims to truth.

The Bible

The Bible is the sacred text of Christians. Christians believe that the Bible is the Word of God – it contains the truth of God. However, Christians do not all agree on whether the Bible is **literally** God's words or not. **Fundamentalist** Christians believe that people who were directly inspired by God wrote the Bible. Every word in the Bible is direct from God, so the truth of God's wishes is very clear.

Liberal Christians disagree. They say people who were inspired by God and their faith wrote the Bible, but that God did not dictate it. The Bible has to be interpreted for the modern world. The truth is in the Bible, but it has to be searched for.

Religious authorities

Religious authority is important as a source of truth, since it is the leaders of a religious tradition that set out teachings and interpret sacred texts. There are many different Christian traditions: Catholic, Orthodox, Church of England (Anglican) and Methodist. Most of the different traditions have formed because of disagreements about religious authority.

For example, the Protestant Churches were formed after people split away from the Catholic Church. These people thought church leaders were more concerned with wealth and power than with following Jesus' teachings. But in the next century, some Christians thought the leaders of the Protestant Churches were *also* getting in the way of the truth of God's message. The non-conformist traditions began to be formed and these traditions believe that everyone is equal before God. The leader is trained to help the people to understand the Christian message and how to live as God would wish.

The leader is often called 'minister' or 'pastor' because of this role as guide or helper. Some Christian traditions do not have priests of ministers. For example, the Quakers (Society of Friends) believe that when an individual feels moved to speak in an act or worship, he or she is ministering to others in the group.

The Pope is the leader of the Catholic Church

Individual conscience

As well as teachings and guidance given by sacred texts and religious authorities, Christians follow their own conscience, too. Many Christians believe that our conscience – the feeling inside us that tells us when something is wrong or right – comes from God, or is God.

Test yourself

1 Name a sacred text.
2 Give an example of how the 'truth' of a sacred text is viewed in different ways by **two** religious traditions.
3 What is meant by 'conscience'?
4 (a) Name the leader of the Catholic Church.
(b) Explain the difference between the priest and a minister.

The nature of spirituality

Religious believers may have the inner certainty that God exists, but God is never matter of fact or simply another **material** thing in our material world. Christians, for example, recognise that God must always remain a mystery to them as God is outside time and space and beyond human understanding (**transcendent**).

The opposite of material is spiritual. Many people in our society have a strong desire for wealth and material possessions, but not everyone. There are some people who deliberately choose to live a more spiritual life. Such people decide not to strive for more money to buy more possessions. Some may be religious and will try to live as they think God would wish them to. Some may not be religious, but may decide to devote their lives to the environment, or helping those in need, or simply to living in a different way.

What is spirituality like?

It is very difficult to describe spirituality. There are so many different ways in which people feel spiritual and in which spirituality is expressed. You may have had some spiritual experiences yourself. Some ways to think about the nature of spirituality include:

- 'the meaning of life' – people live day-to-day material lives year in, year out. You are born, grow up, go to school, get a job, have children, retire and die. Every so often, people tend to look outside of the regular patterns of their lives and think a spiritual thought, like: 'Is there any point to it all?'
- feelings of awe, wonder, mystery – again, although most of life is fairly predictable and mundane, every so often something may strike you in a very unusual way. For example, people often feel great awe or wonder at the natural world: a beautiful sunset, perhaps, could cause these feelings.
- inspiration and creativity – there is a spiritual connection to art and creativity. Artists have often said that they have felt inspired by something greater than themselves. It might be God or a connection to other people or the natural world. Many architects have expressed their

spirituality by the construction of magnificent cathedrals and churches in which to worship God. In the Orthodox tradition, special paintings called **icons** are produced and decorate Orthodox Christian homes and churches as an aid to prayer and meditation.

- feeling part of humanity, of the world – materialism is very individual and selfish: we want more things for ourselves. Spiritual experiences may come from helping others, from helping the natural environment, from recognising ourselves as part of something bigger and more important than ourselves.
- closeness to the Divine – this means a feeling of closeness to God. Religious believers strive for this feeling and it is an important part of many religious experiences.

In your course, you will have studied how spirituality is expressed in religious traditions – through worship, helping others, individual piety and creativity, and so on. You will need to know some examples of these to use in your exam. This study guide looks at how spirituality is expressed in the Christian religious traditions on pages 8–11.

First, though, this study guide looked at claims to truth in the Christian traditions.

People sometimes feel awe at the beauty of the natural world

Test yourself

1 What does it mean to describe God as 'transcendent'?
2 Describe what is meant by a 'material' life.
3 Give three examples of 'spiritual' experiences.
4 What is meant by 'closeness to the Divine'?

Spirituality in society 1

The previous two pages looked at the nature of spirituality. You also need to know about how two religious traditions express their spirituality. There are three main ways through which religious believers do this:

- **individual commitment**
- **supporting voluntary organisations**
- **belonging to a faith community.**

These two pages and the following two look at these three areas in a bit more detail.

Revision tip

You need to refer to **two** religious traditions when answering questions about spirituality in society. These two pages look at differences within Christian traditions. You may have different examples to use as well as or instead of these.

Prayer is not only speaking to God but also listening for a reply

For a Christian, faith means more than simply believing that God exists. It means that they must trust in the love of God and God's support in their lives. Christians hope to draw closer to God. They also wish to express their belief and trust in God. Christians, like other religious believers, express these feelings through worship. These acts of **piety** (devotion to God) may be in private or in public.

Individual commitment

Some Christians will withdraw from everyday life for a time to give their full attention to God and Jesus. This is called 'going on retreat'. Other Christians may believe that they have a spiritual calling – a **vocation**. This could be to leave their daily lives and become a monk or nun so that they can spend much of each day seeking to get closer to God without the distractions of daily life. Or their vocation might be to serve God by becoming a teacher, a doctor, a lawyer, and so on.

Most Christians express their spirituality through private prayer and studying the Bible. For some Christians, **symbolism** plays an important part in public and private worship. The symbol reminds them of an aspect of belief and helps them to concentrate on God and Jesus. For example, many Christians use a cross or a crucifix to help them to think about the death and resurrection of Jesus. In public worship there are some differences between the

Christian traditions over symbolism. For example, non-conformist churches do not agree with the rituals of other churches and do not use the symbolism of bread and wine as the body and blood of Christ. (See the next two pages also.)

Supporting voluntary organisations

Many Christians believe that they can follow the teaching of Jesus by helping people less fortunate than themselves. This may include raising money to support the work of charities seeking to overcome problems or working full time for an organisation. For example, some Christians work in developing countries to help overcome the poverty there.

Quakers (Society of Friends) believe that worship and social action cannot be separated from helping others as a way of worshipping God. Christianity teaches that people cannot be true believers if they do nothing to help the poor.

Revision tip

Aids to prayer that some Christians use include the rosary, statues and icons. Knowing the details of how Christians use such aids to prayer will be useful for answering exam questions about the nature of spirituality.

Test yourself

1 (a) What is piety?
  (b) Give an example of an act of piety.
2 (a) Why do some Christians 'go on retreat'?
  (b) Why do some Christians become monks or nuns?
3 (a) What is a symbol?
  (b) Why do you think many religious believers use symbols as part of their worship?
4 (a) Why do some Christians believe that they should help those in need?
  (b) How might Christians express their spirituality through voluntary work to help those in need?

Spirituality in society 2

Corporate worship

Most religious believers will meet with others who share their beliefs for an act of public (corporate) worship. This is an important way of expressing their love for God. Corporate worship is a public expression of faith.

Being part of a faith community also has some important benefits for believers, as well as some responsibilities. For example, worshipping along with other people who believe the same thing helps strengthen people's faith and it also means people learn more about their faith and its teachings. Faith communities try to help each other and their wider community, which is a big responsibility, but one many believers find very rewarding.

There are many forms of corporate worship within Christianity. The form of worship is influenced by the beliefs of the denomination to which the Christian belongs.

Most Christians believe that the Bible is the Word of God and it is used in most forms of Christian worship. However, the focus given to the Bible in worship varies from tradition to tradition. For example:

- In the **non-conformist churches** the Bible is the main focus of the worship and it is believed that salvation can be achieved by living by the truth as contained in the Bible.
- **Catholics** and **Orthodox** Christians believe that the way to salvation is through the consecrated bread and wine of the Holy Communion service. These two religious traditions believe that the bread and wine become the actual body and blood of Christ when consecrated (blessed) by the priest. This means that readings from the Bible are not the central forms of corporate worship in these traditions.

Two very different forms of Christian worship are found in the Catholic Church and the Society of Friends (Quakers).

The Society of Friends (Quakers)

The Society of Friends does not celebrate Holy Communion. They believe that communion with God is an inward grace brought through the gift of the Holy Spirit and no outward action is needed. The main features of a Quaker meeting are:

- no formal service or hymn singing
- no ordained leader of the service
- worshippers sit quietly meditating until someone feels moved by the Holy Spirit to speak (a **ministry**)
- someone may feel moved to say a prayer or read a section of the Bible or a poem
- after an hour, one of the leaders of the group brings the service to an end.

The Catholic Mass

The Catholic Church teaches that the Mass (Holy Communion) is the most important act of worship. Catholics believe that Christ is present and his sacrifice is repeated at each Mass. The main features of the Mass are:

- a formal service with hymns, readings and special prayers at particular points in the service
- one leader of the worship – the priest
- the priest leads the service. He asks the Holy Spirit to make the bread and wine become the actual body and blood of Christ (**transubstantiation**) and he gives the communion wafer and the wine (if it is given) to the congregation
- the congregation respond to the priest's words at set points in the service: they shake hands with each other (**the sign of peace**) and go up to the altar to receive communion.

Test yourself

1 What is corporate worship?
2 What are the benefits of corporate worship to religious believers?
3 Choose **two** different religious traditions and describe their acts of corporate worship.

Section B

Religious responses to … contemporary issues

The sanctity of life

Words you need to know

- **Sanctity of life** is the view that life is sacred because God has given it.

Revision tip

You need to refer to **two** religious traditions when answering questions about matters of life. This unit looks at differences within Christian traditions. You may have different examples to use as well as or instead of these.

Most religious people believe that life comes from God and is therefore sacred. This is called the 'sanctity of life' and includes the beliefs that:

- God creates all human beings as individuals with the right to life
- every individual is unique
- human beings have a special place in God's eyes and in God's creation.

God as creator of life

Christian beliefs about God as creator include the belief that all human beings are created as individuals. Every individual is unique and unlike any other individual in the universe. God is responsible for each life and has decided each person's identity before he or she was born. Human beings have a special place in God's eyes and in God's creation. For Christians, human beings are made in the image, or likeness, of God: 'So God created human beings, making them like himself' (**Genesis 1:27**).

Psalm 138:13–16 says that God created every part of a human being and that God knows the identity of each person before they are born.

When does life begin?

Christians agree that God is the creator of life, but often disagree at which stage in the pregnancy life begins.

Catholics believe that life begins at the moment of conception when the sperm fertilises the ovum.

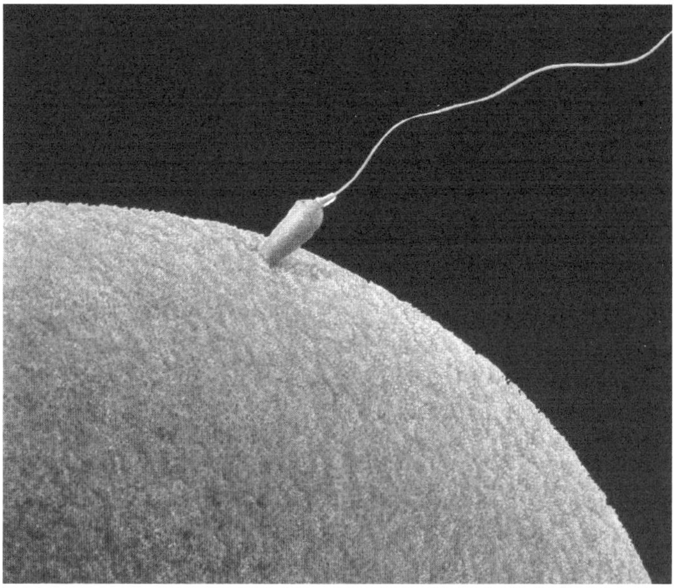

Is this the moment at which life begins?

The Church of England teaches that life begins at about fourteen days when the first anatomical feature, the **primitive steak**, appears. Prior to this point, the embryo can split into more than one individual and therefore the Church argues that up to that point, the embryo cannot be a distinct human being.

Other Christians have different views about when life begins. Some believe it is the moment of implantation when the fertilised egg (**blastocyst**) becomes attached to the mother's womb. Others would say it is when the embryo's heart begins to beat or movement first takes place, or even at the moment of birth when the child takes his or her first independent breath.

Revision tip

Keep up to date on what is happening in the news on human fertilisation. An up-to-date case study on this topic may help you with an examination answer.

Test yourself

1 What is meant by the 'sanctity of life'?
2 How might a religious believer apply the teachings of Genesis 1:27 and Psalm 138:13–16 to issues related to the sanctity of life?
3 Why is deciding on when life begins important for religious believers?
4 Give an example of **two** religious traditions that do not agree on when life begins.

Fertility treatment

Words you need to know

- **AID** is when the mother's egg is fertilised with a donor's sperm because her partner is infertile. AID means artificial insemination by donor.
- **AIH** is when the husband's sperm is artificially placed inside the woman. AIH means artificial insemination by husband.
- **Embryology** is the study of embryos.
- ***In vitro*** fertilisation (IVF) is the fertilisation of the ovum outside the womb.
- **Surrogacy** is when a woman has a baby for another woman who is infertile.

Revision tip

Test-tube baby is a term used to describe a baby produced by IVF. The first 'test-tube baby' was called Louise Brown. She was born in 1978.

Infertility is a common problem in our society and different procedures have been developed to help couples who cannot conceive through normal intercourse to have children.

- ***In vitro*** **fertilisation (IVF)** is when the ovum is fertilised in a 'test tube' and then implanted in the woman's womb. The ovum may be the woman's or donated from another woman. The ovum is then fertilised by the sperm of the woman's husband. If both partners are infertile then an embryo may be donated and implanted. Embryos can now be produced by IVF and frozen until a woman wishes to have a baby.
- **AIH** is the use of artificial methods to put the husband's sperm into the woman.
- **AID** is used when a woman's male partner is infertile and a donor's sperm is used instead.
- **Surrogacy** is when a woman bears the child for a woman who cannot become pregnant. The woman may become pregnant through the implantation of a fertilised egg from the couple seeking to have a child, or from donated sperm from the husband, or egg from the wife.

The Human Fertilisation and Embryology Act 1990 regulates IVF. It also sets out conditions for surrogacy, including the right for the surrogate mother not to have to give up the baby. The couple having a surrogate baby have to be married, over eighteen, and have to provide either the sperm or the ovum of the surrogate. Surrogacy is regulated by the Surrogacy Arrangements Act 1985. This act makes it an offence to advertise surrogacy services or for a company or agency to be paid for arranging the surrogacy.

Christian attitudes to fertility treatment

Although Christians believe that children are a gift from God and one of the purposes of marriage is reproduction, not all Christians agree with fertility treatment for childless couples. Some Christians believe that it is against the will of God to use artificial insemination. These Christians believe a couple should leave the decision as to whether or not they have children to God.

The Catholic Church teaches that children should only be conceived from natural intercourse within marriage. Any other method goes against God's will. **Pope Pius XII** condemned AID and surrogacy because 'a third person becoming involved in a marriage is like "mechanical adultery"' (the seventh commandment is 'You shall not commit adultery'). The Church, therefore, only allows IVF and AIH under the following conditions.

- No 'spare' embryos are produced, as life begins at the moment of conception.
- The sperm and the egg belong to the married couple.
- IVF and AIH are not used instead of sexual intercourse between the husband and wife.

The Church of England allows the use of IVF as long as it only involves a married couple and 'the treatment should normally be given to women during years, when under normal circumstances, they might conceive' (**General Synod, 1997**). The Church of England is against surrogacy, as it teaches that it is wrong to pay a woman to bear a child for another.

Most Protestants accept AIH and IVF as long as it only involves a married couple and there is no third person involved, as they share the Catholic view that this could be classed as 'adultery'.

Test yourself

1. Explain what is meant by IVF and state why it is used.
2. How might religious teachings on the sanctity of life influence attitudes to fertility treatment?
3. Choose **two** different religious traditions and outline the teachings of each about fertility treatment.

Genetic engineering

Human genetic engineering is a very fast-moving area of medical science. The genes that cause or contribute to a wide range of diseases and conditions have now been identified. Technology to replicate genes through cloning is advanced. There are many moral issues related to human genetic engineering.

Words you need to know *

- **Blood transfusion** is giving someone blood from another person, for example, during operations.
- **Cloning** is the production of individuals that are genetically identical.
- **Embryology** is the study of embryos.
- **Genetic engineering** is the alteration of genes to produce a particular effect.
- **Transplant surgery** is surgery that replaces organs or tissue from one individual with that from another.

Some Christians believe that the work of the genetic engineers may be going against God's plan for the world and fear that scientists are seeking to put themselves in the place of God. Other Christians argue that as God made us in 'his image', God has given us the ability to learn and develop. Genetic engineering may be part of God's plan for human development.

Embryology

Embryo research is an important part of genetic engineering. Under the Human Fertilisation and Embryology Act 1990, scientists can use human embryos up until the embryos are fourteen days old for research into fertility, contraception, miscarriages, congenital diseases and chromosome abnormalities. The law does not allow the use of embryos for research into diseases. In February 2002, British scientists were allowed the use of embryonic stem cells as a source of spare body tissue for transplants and the cloning of embryos in the laboratory for medical research.

The Catholic Church believes life begins at the moment of conception and therefore embryos are human beings made in the image of God and possessing a soul. The Catholic Church teaches that embryology is a sin.

Many Christians are concerned that embryos could become a financial commodity, bought and sold for experimental use. These Christians feel that this would be exploitation and against God's teaching. The Church of England is against the production of embryos specifically for research and does not believe any embryos should be used after they are fourteen days old. The Methodist Church supports genetic engineering if it is used to improve the health of the world, but not if it is used to exploit anyone.

The cloning of a sheep has raised the possibility that humans could be cloned

Cloning

Cloning is an aspect of genetic engineering that allows for the reproduction of identical creatures or the growing of new tissue. Embryo cloning uses cells from an embryo to create another identical embryo. Therapeutic cloning uses embryo stem cells from one individual to grow new tissue for another individual. Embryo cloning has produced cloned animals and human cloning is now technically possible, though illegal in many countries, including the UK.

Most Christians believe that each person has a special relationship with God and is created as an individual. Therefore they are strongly opposed to the cloning of human beings. These Christians believe cloning goes against the sanctity of life. There are other objections: research into cloning requires many embryos, most of which are not fertilised and are discarded. Cloning research also tends to produce some abnormalities before a full clone is developed.

Revision tip

Jehovah's Witnesses are a Christian religious tradition that do not allow blood transfusions. They follow the Bible teaching that blood should not be consumed (**Leviticus 17:10–11**).

Blood transfusions and transplant surgery

Many Christians choose to make blood and organ donations, even if the organs are transplanted after their death. This is because blood transfusions and the transplant of organs seek to preserve life. They are regarded as ways of helping the sick. Helping the sick was one of the actions that Jesus praised in the Parable of the Sheep and the Goats (**Matthew 25:31–46**).

Test yourself

1. What is genetic engineering?
2. What is cloning? Is human cloning permitted in the UK?
3. Explain the views of **two** different religious traditions on embryology.

When does life end?

Words you need to know

- **Sanctity of life** is the view that life is sacred because God has given it.
- **Life-support machines** keep people alive when they would otherwise have died.

Revision tip

You need to refer to **two** religious traditions when answering questions about matters of death. This unit looks at differences within Christian traditions. You may have different examples to use as well as or instead of these.

The belief in the **sanctity of life** means that Christians have to decide not only when life begins but also when life ends. In the past, people were declared dead when their heart stopped beating. However, advances in medical science have meant that it is possible to keep a person's heart beating by machine and so a new definition of death had to be introduced. A person is now declared 'brain dead' when there is no response to any form of stimulus.

The advances in medical science have left some people alive but with a quality of life that many people regard as no life at all. For example, there are people who are in what is called a 'permanent vegetative state'. These people are able to breathe for themselves but have no awareness of their identity or their surroundings. They have to be artificially fed. There are other people who are kept alive by **life-support machines** and if the machine failed then they would die. People question whether such people are truly alive.

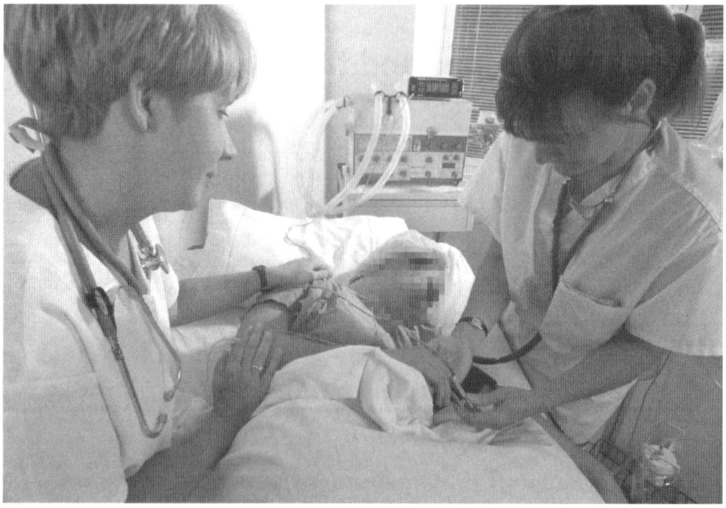

Are people that are kept alive by a machine truly alive?

Life after death

An individual's views on when people should be allowed to die may well be affected by their beliefs about life after death.

Christians believe that death is only the continuation of an eternal life. Many Christians believe that this is with God for those who have accepted Christ. In the **Apostles' Creed**, Christians state that they believe that after death there will be the 'resurrection of the body' and 'life everlasting'. Most Christians are comforted that when loved ones die they will be with God in heaven and that all their suffering in this world has ended.

Most Christians believe that God judges them on their actions in life and they must try to avoid any action that might result in God's punishment. Some Christian traditions, for example, the **Calvinists**, believe that God has already decided who will go to heaven and who will not. Most Christian traditions, however, say that God will forgive sins and it is up to people's actions and beliefs as to whether they go to heaven or not.

In the past, most Christians were very afraid of hell as a real place of torment and suffering. Now, not all Christians believe hell is a real place. Most do believe that the souls of those who are not saved will be without God, however. Catholics and Orthodox Christians often believe in purgatory: a place where souls are purified until they are ready to go to heaven. Protestant believers do not accept that purgatory exists.

Test yourself

1. Explain the term 'brain dead'.
2. How does 'sanctity of life' come into discussions about when people should be allowed to die?
3. Describe the views of two religious traditions about life after death.

Euthanasia 1

Words you need to know

- **Euthanasia** is the practice of ending the life of people who are suffering, using painless methods.
- **Voluntary euthanasia** occurs when a person requests death to end their suffering and is helped to die.
- **Involuntary euthanasia** occurs when the person has no part in the decision-making process to end their suffering.
- **Passive euthanasia** occurs when no action is taken to prolong life but there is no deliberate action to end the life.
- **Active euthanasia** is when a deliberate action is taken to end a life.
- **Suicide** is taking one's own life.
- A **hospice** is a special type of hospital or home that cares for terminally ill patients.

Euthanasia is a complex topic with many arguments for and against. In this country, it is legal to commit suicide, but it is still illegal to ask someone else to take your life. **Voluntary euthanasia** is legal in some countries, like the Netherlands and Switzerland, for example. Strict regulations control its use. In this country, doctors do give patients who are near death drugs that reduce suffering but also make them die more quickly. UK courts do sometimes allow doctors to turn off life-support machines for some brain-dead patients.

Revision tip

The physicist, Stephen Hawking, has motor neurone disease. He was diagnosed in his early 20s and was not expected to live more than a few more years. Many years later, he is still making very important scientific discoveries. Some Christians would argue this is an example of God having plans for people even when medical science had written them off.

Christian attitudes against euthanasia

Most Christians believe that God is the giver of life and it is up to God to make the decision when a life ends, not humans. Biblical teachings to support this include the following.

- 'Do not commit murder' is the sixth commandment (**Exodus 20:12**).
- **Deuteronomy 30:19** says people have a choice between life and death and that people should choose life.
- **Acts 17:26** says that God has fixed how long people are to live.
- St Paul taught that because Jesus died to save the world from sin then people cannot do as they wish: 'you are not

your own' (**1 Corinthians 6:19**). 'If we live, we are responsible to the Lord, and when we die we are responsible to the Lord. Both in life and in death we belong to the Lord.' (**Romans 14:18**)

- St Paul also taught that the human body is a 'temple to God' and it is wrong to destroy God's temple (**1 Corinthians 3:16**).

The Catholic Church opposes all forms of euthanasia. It sees involuntary euthanasia as murder and voluntary euthanasia as being **suicide**, which is a sin. Life is God-given and sacred.

Catholics and many other Christians from other religious traditions might also use the following arguments against euthanasia.

- Suffering is terrible, but it is a way of strengthening faith and is there for a purpose: it is part of God's plan, which we cannot know.
- Euthanasia shows a lack of faith in God. The chance of a cure or miracle is removed if euthanasia takes place.
- Helping the sick, disabled, and elderly teaches compassion. It offers the chance to put Christian teaching into practise.
- God may have plans for people even when it appears that their life is finished.

The Hospice Movement

The Hospice Movement aims to provide care for people who are dying. Pain relief is part of this, but also emotional care to help people deal with the fear of death and to die in dignity. Many Christians believe that hospices help some people combat the temptation of euthanasia.

Revision tip

Dame Cicely Saunders started the Hospice Movement. Knowing more about the work of the Hospice Movement will help you to answer questions about euthanasia.

Dame Cicely Saunders started the Hospice Movement

Test yourself

1 Explain the difference between voluntary and involuntary euthanasia.

2 Is passive euthanasia illegal in the UK?

3 (a) Explain why the Catholic Church opposes voluntary and involuntary euthanasia.
(b) What religious teachings might the Catholic Church use to support its view?
(c) Why would Catholics be likely to support the work of hospices?

Euthanasia 2

Words you need to know *

Quality of life is a measure of the capacity someone has to experience life rather than just 'be alive'.

Christian attitudes in support of euthanasia rights

Pages 22–23 looked at Christian arguments against euthanasia. Although they view life as a gift from God, some Christians believe that people who are suffering should have the right to die with dignity and support euthanasia.

While many Christians would oppose **active euthanasia** as being murder, some Christians accept **passive euthanasia** as it is placing the choice as to whether the person lives or dies in God's hands. They accept that the painkillers given to ease the suffering of terminally ill patients can hasten death, but do not regard this as a deliberate action to kill the person. Other Christians do support active enthanasia. These Christians might argue that God has given people intelligence and the freedom to make choices about their life. Also, God would not want people to suffer when they did not need to.

When making moral decisions related to issues such as euthanasia, religious believers consider not only the sanctity of a life but also the **quality of life**. Quality of life is not how rich a person is or how many possessions they have: it is whether they are aware of themselves and the world they live in and the degree of pain and suffering a person may be experiencing. Some Christians believe **involuntary euthanasia** should be legal so that the lives of people in permanent vegetative states can be ended, as there is no quality of life.

The arguments of Christians in favour of euthanasia include the following.

- People should be allowed to decide for themselves when they want to die. Suicide is legal so why not euthanasia?
- Life comes from God, but there is nothing in the Bible that states that a person must be kept alive at any cost. It is wrong to artificially preserve life beyond its natural span and this may be going against God's plan: 'He sets

the time for birth and the time for death...the time for killing and the time for healing.' (**Ecclesiastes 3:1–3**)

- Keeping people alive by machine or in a permanent vegetative state is not life in the true sense. Jesus said: 'I have come that you might have life – life in all its fullness' (**John 10:10**) and so some Christians argue that if this is not possible then people have the right to die.

Suicide

Many people regard voluntary euthanasia as assisted suicide. Many Christians believe that although suicide is legal, it is not what God wants. Life is a gift from God and however difficult life becomes it is not for people to decide to end it. **Acts 17:26** states that God has fixed our life span and therefore suicide would be against God's plan. Many Christians believe that it shows a lack of faith and trust in God's good purpose. St Paul taught that God would give no more suffering than people can cope with and they must accept what happens.

Quakers believe that 'every stage of our lives offers fresh opportunities' and so whatever happens in life people should learn from it. If, however, someone commits suicide, Quakers do not believe that they have the right to condemn them. Many Christians now share the views of the Quakers. Most Christians will seek to do everything possible to help a person considering taking their own life.

Revision tip

Many Christians support the work of the Samaritans as they believe that if people have someone to talk to there is less risk of them taking their own life. Knowing some details of the work of the Samaritans could be useful in answering questions about attitudes to suicide.

Test yourself

1. Explain what is meant by 'quality of life'.
2. Why might people who support the right to involuntary euthanasia use 'quality of life' as part of their argument?
3. What reasons might a religious believer give for supporting involuntary euthanasia? Try to give some religious teachings in your answer.
4. Give an example of two different religious attitudes to suicide.

Care of the sick and the elderly

One function of the family is to meet the human needs of love and companionship. The family provides an economic unit in which everyone is supported from birth until death, including the sick, disabled and the elderly.

The **nuclear family** is usually one or two adults living with their own or adopted children. The **extended family** includes grandparents, aunts and uncles, as well as nephews, nieces and cousins. In many societies the extended family live together and take the shared responsibility of bringing up the children, caring for the sick and elderly members of the family, and sharing expenses. There is always someone to turn to when things go wrong as well as sharing all the family celebrations.

In modern Britain the job market means that many people move away from their family and so the family support is no longer available. The result is that many sick, disabled and elderly people have to depend on the local authorities rather than their families for care.

Elderly people, for example, may be provided with carers to visit them in their homes or placed in sheltered accommodation or residential homes. Local authorities also provide nursing homes, where residents receive the medical care they need.

Christians believe that the teaching of Jesus makes it clear that they have a duty to help the sick, disabled and elderly, and support the work of charities trying to improve such people's quality of life. Christians believe that they have a duty to care for the elderly as God commands them to 'Honour their father and their mother' (**Exodus 20:12**). Many churches collect food at their harvest festival service for the elderly as well as organising social events for them.

In the past, families lived near to each other and it was easy for people to look after their parents and to keep the fifth commandment. Unfortunately, work commitments have resulted in many people having to move away from their parents. They have had to set up home in another part of the UK, or even abroad, and it has become impossible for them to care for their aged parents.

The result is that many elderly people who can no longer lead independent lives have to go into sheltered accommodation or residential homes, where they are cared for by qualified people instead of members of their family. Many Christians support the work of organisations that care for the elderly, like Help the Aged, or visit elderly people in their locality. Many churches collect food at their harvest festival service to distribute to the elderly, as well as organising social events for them.

Test yourself

1. What is a nuclear family?
2. What is an extended family?
3. What differences will there be between a trained nurse caring for an elderly man and a loving daughter caring for her aged father? Give reasons for your answer.
4. Why do you think that many Christians help elderly people to have a better quality of life?

Drugs and the law 1

Words you need to know

- A **drug** is a substance that can alter a person's mind and/or body systems.
- **Social drugs** are taken as part of social events, for example, drinking with friends. Some social drugs are legal, some are used illegally.
- **Recreational drugs** can include legal drugs, but the term is mostly used to describe illegal drugs that are a major part of a 'recreational' activity, like dancing.

Legal drugs

Some drugs are legally acceptable, for example, caffeine, nicotine and alcohol.

Coffee, tea, cola-flavoured drinks and chocolate contain the drug **caffeine**. Caffeine is a stimulant that makes a person feel more energetic. It is addictive and does have some side effects, but these are not thought to be serious to health. There are no laws against the purchase of products containing caffeine.

Coffee, tea, cola-flavoured drinks and chocolate all contain the drug caffeine

Nicotine is the addictive drug found in tobacco. It is illegal to buy tobacco in Britain under sixteen years of age. Cigarettes carry a health warning because it is known that smoking causes lung cancer and heart disease as well as other respiratory problems. These diseases are often fatal. Every year the treatment of smoking-related illnesses costs the National Health Service (NHS) over £400 million.

Alcohol is a drug. Alcohol cannot be legally purchased by anyone under eighteen years of age. Although alcohol appears to be a stimulant, it is in fact a depressive drug. This can make heavy alcohol users violent, sometimes suicidal.

Alcohol misuse contributes significantly to crime levels through alcohol specific offences, for example, being drunk and disorderly in public. It has been estimated that 40 per cent of violent crime, 78 per cent of assaults, and 88 per cent of criminal damage cases are committed while the offender is under the influence of alcohol. One in seven road deaths are the result of drink driving.

Excessive drinking of alcohol can damage the brain and liver as well as cause heart disease, strokes and cancer. Alcoholics are addicted to alcohol and find that the compulsion to drink often ruins not only their health but also their life.

Tobacco products and alcohol are heavily taxed in this country. Some of the revenue raised from these taxes is used to support medical research and the National Health Service. Many people argue that the cost of the treatment of people for their use of these two drugs is greater than the money raised.

Revision tip

It would be useful for the exam to know about the work of an organisation that seeks to overcome the problems of addiction to drugs or alcohol, like Alcoholics Anonymous, for example.

Test yourself

1 What is a drug?

2 Give three examples of drugs that are legal in this country.

3 (a) Describe the effects of caffeine, nicotine and alcohol.
(b) What are the legal controls on the sale of tobacco products and alcohol?
(c) Give **two** examples of the problems smoking and alcohol abuse cause society.

Drugs and the law 2

Revision tip

For your exam, you need to know about the effects legal and illegal drugs produce and what the mental, physical and legal consequences of taking them can be. The information in the study guide is only basic. Make sure you know the details, too.

Illegal drugs

Illegal drugs are classified according to how dangerous they are.

Class A drugs

Class A drugs include heroin, cocaine and crack cocaine, Ecstasy and LSD.

- All produce a mental high. LSD produces hallucinations.
- All have strong physical effects. Cocaine and LSD increase blood pressure and heart rate and users often experience disorientation, as do Ecstasy users. Heroin often produces constipation and appetite loss.
- All carry serious health risks. Heroin and cocaine (especially crack cocaine) are highly addictive and overdosing is often fatal. Ecstasy has been linked to deaths through overheating (dehydration) and damage to the brain, liver and kidneys. LSD can cause coma and convulsions, and LSD and heroin use can both lead to mental health problems.
- Possession of Class A drugs carries a maximum punishment of seven years in prison and/or a heavy fine. Supplying them can mean life imprisonment and/or a heavy fine.

Class B drugs

Class B drugs include cannabis and amphetamines. If amphetamines are injected they become Class A.

- Cannabis/marijuana produces a mental high and feeling of relaxation and being more sociable. Amphetamines produce a 'rush', a feeling of increased energy and speed.
- Physical effects of cannabis use include increased heart rate, increased appetite, loss of short-term memory. The effects of amphetamine use include increased heart rate, tiredness and depression after use.
- The health risks of cannabis use has been linked to the same health problems as suffered by smokers, including

lung cancer (even when the drug is not smoked with tobacco). High doses of amphetamines cause panic attacks and hallucinations. Long-term use can cause mental illness and heart problems.

- The maximum penalty for possession is five years in prison and/or a fine. The maximum penalty for supplying the drug is fourteen years in prison and/or a fine.

Class C drugs

Class C drugs include tranquillisers and anabolic steroids. Anabolic steroids are also types of **performance enhancing drugs**.

- Tranquillisers have a calming effect and reduce anxiety. Anabolic steroids enable people to train harder, build muscle faster, and are used by athletes.
- Tranquillisers can affect memory; anabolic steroids can produce feelings of aggression.
- The health risks of tranquillisers is that they can be addictive and are very dangerous, when mixed with alcohol. With anabolic steroids, women may develop more facial hair, deeper voice, and there is also a risk of miscarriage. Men may develop impotence and sterility, and there are heart and liver risks, too.
- For anabolic steroids and tranquillisers, possession is not illegal but supply is.
- As performance enhancing drugs have been banned in sport, athletes will be tested for anabolic steroids before major competitions. A positive test will disqualify an athlete from a sport, often for many years.

Test yourself

1 Describe the effects of **two** Class A drugs.
2 What are the health risks of **two** Class B drugs?
3 What are the maximum legal penalties for possessing and of supplying Class A drugs?

Debate over drugs

Drugs are often classed as being 'hard' or 'soft'. There are debates about legalising both hard drugs and soft drugs.

Hard drugs

Hard drugs are Class A drugs and they are addictive drugs. These drugs not only lead to ill health or even the death of addicts, but also cause many addicts to commit crimes to get the money they need to support their habit. Many thieves and prostitutes are addicts, who break the law to buy drugs such as heroin or cocaine. The problems associated with the illegal use of hard drugs have led to people considering their legalisation.

Arguments for legalising hard drugs

- Hard drugs have a high street value because they are 'very' illegal as well as highly addictive. If they were legalised and the supply controlled then addicts would not need to commit crimes to get the drug.
- If there are no more massive profits in drug trafficking then the drug system that encourages pushers to get more and more people addicted would break up.
- Addicts would no longer fear admitting their addiction and would seek help.
- The police would be freed from drug enforcement to deal with other crimes.

Arguments against legalising hard drugs

- Hard drugs are very dangerous to health and so society has a duty to stop them being used.
- It would send out the message that drug taking is acceptable and more people will take them.
- If hard drugs are legal then there is a greater risk of young people becoming addicted to them.

Soft drugs

Drugs that are not physically addictive are called soft drugs. Cannabis is the soft drug that causes the most debate. Some people want it to be legalised.

Arguments for legalising cannabis

- Cannabis is not physically addictive and is less harmful than alcohol, which is legal.
- Cannabis is helpful in relieving the suffering of people with illnesses like multiple sclerosis.
- Legalising cannabis would free up police to deal with more serious offences.

Some people campaign for cannabis to be legalised

Arguments against legalising cannabis

- The long-term effects of taking cannabis could be harmful and are not, as yet, known.
- Cannabis can lead people on to take hard drugs.
- Cannabis can cause dangerous driving, like alcohol – but it also stays in the body longer than alcohol.
- There is evidence that people become psychologically dependent on cannabis.

Revision tip

In July 2002, the UK government proposed that cannabis be changed from a Class B drug to a Class C drug. This had not been made law when this book was being written – but it might be now! The proposed changes **do not mean** cannabis is going to become a legal drug. There will still be penalties for possessing and supplying cannabis.

Test yourself

1 (a) Why do some people believe that the sale of hard drugs should be legalised?
  (b) Why are other people opposed to the legalisation of the sale of hard drugs?
2 (a) Why do some people believe that the sale of cannabis should be legalised?
  (b) Why are other people opposed to the legalisation of cannabis?

Christian attitudes to drugs

Illegal drugs

Most Christians are opposed to the use of illegal drugs. St Paul taught that the authority of the State must be obeyed as God put it there. If the State makes an action illegal then St Paul taught that to break that law would be to go against God and it therefore becomes a sin (**Romans 13:1–5**).

More importantly, perhaps, is the teaching of St Paul about how people should treat their bodies. In **1 Corinthians 3:16–17** he said that the body is 'God's temple' and that the Holy Spirit from God works within people. He warned that 'if anyone destroys God's temple, God will destroy him. For God's temple is holy, and you yourselves are his temple.' Many Christians would see the use of illegal drugs as going directly against God's wishes for how people should treat their bodies.

Legal drugs

Adults may legally smoke and drink alcohol in the UK, but many Christians believe that tobacco should be avoided because of the health risks, not only to themselves but also to others.

Different Christian religious traditions have different perspectives on the use of alcohol. Some Christian traditions, like the Quakers, Methodists, Baptists and Salvation Army, have always been opposed to alcohol because of the serious social and health problems it can cause. The Salvation Army, for example, started at a time when poor people lived miserable lives and used alcohol as a way of escape from their problems – leading to violence, debt and more misery. Every Salvationist makes a commitment to live an alcohol-free life.

There are Christian teachings against alcohol. St Paul reminded Christians in **Romans 13:13** that they must not indulge in 'orgies and drunkenness…' **Ephesians 5:18** says: 'Do not get drunk with wine, for that is debauchery.' However, St Paul also told his friend Timothy that wine could help him overcome illness: 'Stop drinking only water, and use a little wine because of your stomach and your frequent illnesses.' (**1 Timothy 5:23**) Most Christians would

Revision tip

You need to be able to refer to **two** religious traditions in answers about religious attitudes to drugs.

agree that these teachings oppose alcohol abuse, not alcohol itself.

Most **Catholics** and members of the **Church of England** (Anglicans) would argue that alcohol is acceptable. They use alcoholic wine during their services of Holy Communion as Jesus used alcoholic wine, and it provides a direct link with the event. Also, Jesus' first miracle was to turn water into wine during the celebration of the marriage at Cana (**John 2:1–10**). This does not mean, of course, that these traditions encourage people to drink to excess.

Performance related drugs

Christians believe that God gives everyone special skills (talents). A Christian needs to discover these skills and use them to serve God. Therefore, using performance enhancing drugs is wrong and is a form of cheating. St Paul told people that if they were to win the prize they must 'run a straight race'.

Most Christians believe that it is clear that whatever their own views on drugs may be, they have a duty to help those who have a problem with addiction. Many individual Christians give up time to work in centres helping people with drug problems.

What is your example ... ?

It would be useful for the exam to know about the work of a religious individual or organisation on problems of drug addiction. For example, David Wilkerson's Christian vocation led him to work with the violent teenage gangs of New York. He succeeded in saving many of them from a life of drug addiction and crime and set up the organisation Teen Challenge. What is your example?

Test yourself

1 (a) Why do Baptists use non-alcoholic wine during their Holy Communion service?
  (b) Why do Catholics use alcoholic wine during their Holy Communion service?
2 Why do many Christians believe that they should help those addicted to drugs?
3 Give an account of the work of a religious believer or organisation that seeks to help alcoholics or drug addicts.
4 Why would a Christian be likely to oppose the use of illegal drugs? What teachings might he or she use to support this view?

Media and technology

Words you need to know *

- The **Internet** is a global network that allows access to information on millions of computers worldwide.
- **Terrestrial television** uses transmitters that are on the earth's surface, not in space, to send TV transmissions.
- **Satellite broadcasting** uses satellites in space to send TV transmissions.

There are many forms of media available to most people in the West

The media is the main means of mass communication: it is lots of different ways in which information is passed between people. The forms of media available to most people in the West include newspapers, magazines, radio, terrestrial TV, cinema, music, the Internet and satellite broadcasting.

Access to the media

Most homes in Britain have at least one radio and television. Over 88 per cent of households have a video recorder and CD player. Over 40 per cent of households have satellite, cable and digital receivers. Over a third of households have Internet access.

Newspapers are a very accessible form of media: they are sold everywhere and are cheap to buy. **Tabloid** newspapers are the most popular form of newspaper in this country, for example, *The Sun* and *The Mirror*. Millions more tabloid newspapers are sold each day than **broadsheet** newspapers. Broadsheets carry more news and analysis than tabloids and in more detail. Examples would be *The Telegraph* and *The Guardian*. There are also many magazines available. Magazines are aimed at all ages and interests.

The cinema is another popular form of media. Most people have access to a cinema in their neighbourhood and going to the cinema has become a popular leisure activity. There were over 142 million admissions to the cinema in the year 2001.

The media and society

Everyone is affected by the mass media in modern society. It is through these different forms of communication that we hear about current events, new products, fashion, entertainment, and what is happening in the lives of famous people. The media influences what people think or believe, what people buy, what people eat, what people know, and how people dress.

Currently, the average young person spends more than twenty-one hours per week viewing television. On top of this, there is time spent at the cinema, listening to music, watching videos or DVDs, playing computer games, or surfing the Internet. By the time the average teenager leaves school, they will have spent more time watching TV than time studying in the classroom! People also learn about life through the media.

The benefits of the media for society

- It can be used for public information. For example, drink-driving adverts reduced the number of deaths through drink driving.
- Entertainment in the home – a great advantage especially to people who are disabled, ill or elderly.
- It gives people knowledge to form and express their own opinions on issues.
- It makes people aware of injustices. For example, the USA was forced to take notice of the Civil Rights Movement because of worldwide pressure to stop the violence against the protestors.
- It makes the world aware of disasters and of ways to help. For example, the Live Aid concert raised money worldwide to help the starving people of Ethiopia.
- It makes people aware of other cultures and religions in the world and helps break down barriers of prejudice and discrimination.

The Sun is one of the most popular tabloid newspapers

Revision tip

Our society has very open access to media. In other countries people's access is limited – newspapers may be owned by the government, for example. Make sure you understand what is meant by access to media and technology.

Test yourself

1 What is meant by the media?
2 Name **four** different branches of the media.
3 Why are media and technology linked?
4 What are the main differences between a tabloid and a broadsheet newspaper?
5 What are the influences of the media on society?
6 What are the benefits of the media for the world?
7 How has the media been used to raise money for charity work?

Controlling the media

Words you need to know

- **TV watershed** is a set time before which TV programmes need to be suitable for an audience that includes children.
- **Pornography** is the explicit description or exhibition of sexual activity in literature or film and is intended to stimulate sexual feelings.
- **Censorship** is when an official authority alters or reduces access to media information.

Revision tip

Make sure you know about the debate over the effects of media on society and the ways in which the media is controlled.

Media and technology bring many benefits, but people are also concerned about negatives effects, including:

- children having access to unsuitable material, for example, **pornography**, violence, racial and sexual prejudice, offensive language, which could disturb them or have a bad effect on their behaviour.
- media advertising making people buy things that they cannot afford.
- people identifying role models through the media, some of which are not positive. For example, the media's emphasis on body image is often blamed for the increase in anorexia and bulimia cases.
- the media's obsession with violence. Some people think the high levels of violence in films, video games and TV programmes causes people to be more violent in real life.

The concerns about media influences have led to various restrictions on what can and cannot be shown in television programmes, films, and sent over the Internet. Restrictions like these by official bodies is called **censorship**. There are different kinds of restriction on the media.

The British Board of Film Classification categories

U	Universal – suitable for all audiences four years and over
PG	Parental Guidance – general viewing, but some scenes may be unsuitable for some children
12A	No one younger than twelve may see a '12A' film at the cinema unless accompanied by an adult. No one younger than twelve may rent or buy a '12'-rated video
15	No one younger than fifteen may see a '15' film at the cinema. No one younger than fifteen may rent or buy a '15'-rated video
18	No one younger than eighteen may see an '18' film at the cinema. No one younger than eighteen may rent or buy an '18'-rated video
R18	R18 category is a special and legally restricted classification and may only be supplied in licensed sex shops to people eighteen years and over

- Films have different ratings that restrict access on some films to those under certain ages. Films are rated in this way according to the amounts of sex and violence in them.

- The Video Recording Act 1984 regulated the sale of 'video nasties'. These are video films that include scenes of extreme acts of violence.
- Many satellite and digital boxes, videos and computers, are now fitted with a parental lock to limit what children can watch without parental supervision.
- The **TV watershed** ensures that all television programmes screened in Britain before 9pm should be suitable for audiences that include children.
- The Independent Television Commission (ITC) monitors the independent television companies and deals with complaints. The Broadcasting Standards Commission does similar work.
- The Press Complaints Commission deals with complaints against the Press.
- The Obscene Publications Act 1959 and 1964 and The Telecommunications Act 1984 makes it illegal to publish or send obscene or indecent material.
- The Internet Watch Foundation monitors the Internet for potentially illegal items. This includes websites that contain child pornography, for example.

Not everyone agrees with control of the media. Some people doubt that the media has harmful effects – a definite link has never been proven. It has been argued that parents should supervise their children's access to media, not the state. Individual liberty is restricted by censorship – adults should be able to decide what they watch, listen to, or read for themselves.

What is your example … ?

For your exam, make sure you know an example of an organisation that tries to limit what they regard as the harmful effects of the media on society. One example would be mediawatch-uk. This used to be called the National Viewers and Listeners Association and was set up in 1964 by Mary Whitehouse. What is your example?

Test yourself

1. State and explain **three** concerns about the influence of the media.
2. (a) What is censorship?
   (b) Why do many people believe that there should be no censorship of the media?
3. Give an example of an organisation that is concerned about media and technology having some bad effects on society.

Religion and the media

Words you need to know *

- **Evangelists** try to spread understanding of the Christian Gospel.

Songs of Praise is broadcast by the BBC

Religious broadcasting

The BBC is required to broadcast religious programmes. There are a number of reasons for this. The public pay for the BBC through the TV licence. This means the BBC should provide programmes for all the different groups in society, including religious believers. *Songs of Praise* is the best-known BBC religious programme. Radio 4 also broadcasts religious programmes, including a Daily Service. Most BBC religious programming is Christian, but other faiths are also represented. For example, during Ramadan there are often appropriate religious programmes linked to Islam.

The Religious Broadcasting Act 1990 controls religious broadcasting in Britain. The BBC, ITC and the Radio Authority have to make sure that what they broadcast respects the beliefs of listeners and viewers. Programmes must not offend any of the religious views or beliefs of viewers or listeners. All programmes must be accurate and fair and not seek to convert people to a particular belief. **The Central Religious Advisory Committee (CRAC)** advises the BBC, ITC and Radio Authority about policies and coverage.

'Spreading the word'

The major religions of the world have recognised the importance of the media as a means of spreading their message throughout the world. There are many satellite and digital channels dedicated to the spreading of the religious teachings of a particular faith. In Christianity this is known as **televangelism** because people are using the media as **evangelists**.

The major religions have websites and email addresses to help people find out more about their faith. Local places of worship will often have their own web page to give details of times of worship and other activities.

Christianity

Many Christians believe that it is acceptable to use the media as a means of spreading the Christian message.

These Christians believe that using the media is continuing Jesus' command to 'Go you into the world and preach the Gospel to every creature' (**Mark 16:15**). Billy Graham is an example of a famous evangelist who began to use radio broadcasts in the 1960s and now uses many different forms of media to spread his message.

There is some concern, however, that there have been evangelical Christians in the USA who have used televangelism to make money for themselves and have not led the Christian life that they have been preaching. Jimmy and Tamy Fae Bakker were a prime example of corrupt televangelists who used their religious TV show as a means of making money for themselves.

Raise money for charity

Many charities have seen the advantage of using the media for fund raising to support their work. Organisations like Christian Aid and CAFOD have Internet websites to explain their work and circulate videos to schools and churches with the main aim of gaining support. Many organisations advertise for funds in the newspapers and on commercial television and raido.

Revision tip

It will be useful to know specific examples of religious believers who have made use of media and technology. Billy Graham would be one good example, for instance.

Revision tip

It would be useful to know specific examples of the ways in which an organisation has used the media to support its work. Find out about the advertising campaign of an organisation you have studied: Help the Aged would be a good example, for instance.

Test yourself

1 Name a religious programme on television.
2 Why does the BBC broadcast religious programmes?
3 What Act of Parliament controls the way the media talk about religions and religious faith?
4 What are the advantages and disadvantages of televangelism?
5 (a) Why have many charities chosen to use the media to support their work?
  (b) In what ways might charities use the media to support their work?

Religions and control of the media

Words you need to know

- **Blasphemy** is to speak or to treat a religious or sacred subject disrespectfully.

Revision tip

You need to refer to **two** religious traditions in answers about religious attitudes to media and technology. Check back on your notes to see which religious traditions you have studied for this. One way of tackling this might be to compare fundamentalist and liberal positions on media and technology, for example.

As with all moral issues, religious believers use sources of religious authority, like sacred texts and religious teachings, to decide the attitude that they should take to the media and technology. Believers' own consciences also inform their views.

Some Christians use St Paul's teaching in **1 Corinthians 5:1–5** that anyone responsible for 'sexual immorality' in the community should be thrown out of the community because they are going against the teaching of God and Jesus. St Paul reminds people that such behaviour is a sin. In **1 Thessalonians 4:3** St Paul warns people to avoid sexual immorality and 'that each of you should learn to control his own body in a way that is holy and honourable'. Some Christians argue that this would include not looking at nudity in the tabloid newspapers or magazines or watching sex scenes on film or television.

Blasphemy

Christian beliefs have legal protection in this country against **blasphemy**. The last successful prosecution under the blasphemy law was against the publishers of the magazine *Gay News* in 1977, in connection with a poem depicting Christ as a homosexual.

For some believers, religious teachings are true for all times and people. This is sometimes called a **fundamentalist** position. Other believers may interpret religious teachings for their own times and their views on media and technology may change over time. This is often called a **liberal** position.

What many Christians consider blasphemous has changed with time. When the musical *Jesus Christ Superstar* opened in London in the 1970s, it was considered inappropriate by many Christians to make a musical of the life of Jesus. Today, most Christians would regard the musical as an appropriate way of using modern technology to spread the message of the meaning of Jesus' death.

There are now several television comedy programmes, such as *The Vicar of Dibley*, that are based around aspects of

Christian worship and there are many Christians who watch and enjoy these programmes. A few years ago many people would have considered such programmes blasphemous.

The blasphemy laws of Britain only apply to Christianity. The law would not allow the prosecution of Salman Rushdie in connection with his novel *The Satanic Verses* (1989), because it was some leaders of the Islamic faith and not Christianity that regarded the book as blasphemous.

Many people, including some Christians, argue that the laws should be changed to include those of all faiths or repealed because they are outdated.

Violence and sex scenes

The major concern of some Christians is the inclusion of scenes of extreme violence into films and television programmes. It is felt that such scenes go against the Chistian belief that people should live together in harmony and seek to overcome their differences using peaceful methods. In the Sermon on the Mount, Jesus taught that a Christian must 'turn the other cheek' and to do everything possible to keep the peace (**Matthew 5:38–48**).

Many Christians are also concerned that the inclusion of explicit sex scenes goes against the teaching of Jesus. It is felt that such scenes might encourage 'lustful thoughts', which were condemned by Jesus in the Sermon on the Mount (**Matthew 5:27–32**) As many of these scenes are acts of adultery, many Christians argue that it is encouraging people to believe that it is acceptable to have affairs and to break the seventh commandment: 'You shall not commit adultery' (**Exodus 20:14**).

Test yourself

1. What is blasphemy?
2. Why might a religious parent stop their child watching violent films?
3. Why might a religious believer be concerned about the inclusion of sex scenes in TV programmes?
4. Give an example of a difference of opinion **two** religious believers might have over the use of blasphemy laws.

Causes of crime

Types of crime

A crime is an action that breaks the law of the land. Types of crime include:

- crimes against the person such as assault, rape or murder
- crimes against property such as fraud, theft or vandalism
- crimes against the state such as selling secrets to a foreign power (treason).

Crime and religion

Religious offences (sins) are not always the same as crimes. Religious believers do regard crimes such as murder or theft as sins – these are often prohibited in religious teachings. The Ten Commandments tell people not to commit murder or to steal, for example. But other actions that are not crimes in law are seen as sins for religious believers. For example, adultery is not illegal in Britain but some Christians consider it a sin because it breaks God's command 'You shall not commit adultery' (**Exodus 20:14**).

Causes of crime

There is disagreement about what causes crime. Different points of view include seeing crime as being caused by **environmental** reasons, **social** reasons and **psychological** reasons.

Statistics show that most people who keep on committing crimes (persistent offenders) are also users of hard drugs. Persistent offenders also tend to be unemployed, do not tend to have educational qualifications and have been in care and are young (under twenty-one). This suggests to some people that environmental reasons are a big cause of crime. These are reasons like poverty, bad education, broken homes and drugs.

However, it is not just people from deprived backgrounds that commit crimes and most people who did not have a good upbringing do not necessarily turn into persistent offenders. One major reason why young people get into

Revision tip

Revise the arguments about the causes of crime. Make sure you know the differences between the environmental, social and psychological arguments. Think about what a religious believer's viewpoint might be, too.

trouble and fail to get a good education is truancy. All children are entitled to go to school however deprived their background may be. So some people say it is social reasons that cause crime, peer pressure to truant from school, or to try illegal drugs, for example.

Some people see psychological reasons as the most important cause of crime. Some psychological problems cause crimes, such as kleptomania (stealing) and pyromania (arson). Reports estimate that 90 per cent of young people in prison suffer from mental health problems. Drug addicts are likely to have 'addictive personalities', which means they are more likely to keep on taking drugs than others. And some people think crime is caused when people are naturally greedy and selfish.

'I want to drive a fast car.'

Test yourself

1 What is a crime?
2 What is a sin?
3 State an action that is regarded by some Christians as a sin but is not a crime in Britain.
4 List three possible causes of crime and explain the differences between them.

Types of punishment

Words you need to know

- **Imprisonment** results from a custodial sentence – going to prison, detention centre, and so on.
- **Life imprisonment** is the most severe custodial sentence.
- **Community service** is a fixed number of hours of unpaid work in the community.

Revision tip

Knowing details of punishments used by the court will help you to answer exam questions related to crime and punishment.

There is no one set punishment for 'breaking the law'. Some crimes are considered more serious than others. The punishment is intended to reflect the severity of the crime. A speeding offence carries a fine whereas a murder carries an automatic sentence of **life imprisonment**. The courts also take into account the particular circumstances of a crime. One crime may have been carefully planned and deliberate; another may have been on the spur of the moment. The severity of the punishment may reflect these circumstances.

Courts have many different types of punishment. Here are some of the main types.

- Custodial sentences: **imprisonment** in prison, detention centres or young offender's institutions.
- A community rehabilitation order: offenders see a probation officer or attend a probation centre on a regular basis. It is hoped that the probation officer can 'advise, assist and befriend' offenders and help them to reform.
- A community punishment order is when the court sets a number of hours (between 40–240 hours) of unpaid work in the community that the offender has to complete as a punishment for their crime. This is sometimes called **community service**.
- Fines: the offender has to pay a sum of money to the court as a punishment for their offence.
- Suspended sentences: only come into effect if the convicted person commits the same offence again.

The age of responsibility

A child under the age of ten will not be charged with breaking the law. This is because a child under ten is not considered old enough to know right from wrong. It is not until the age of fourteen that a child can be given a custodial sentence such as a detention centre. However, if a child under fourteen does commit a serious crime, he or she would be held in a place of safety until it was considered there was no longer a danger from the child to society. A sixteen year old who breaks the law can be sent to a young offender's institution and at eighteen can be sent to prison.

The aims of punishment

All punishments seek to reduce the number of crimes committed, but the way that they aim to achieve this varies. There are five main aims of punishment.

The aim of protection

The punishment is trying to protect society from anti-social behaviour by stopping offenders repeating their actions. A punishment that could be given with the aim of protection is a driving ban for dangerous driving.

The aim of retribution (revenge)

The punishment is intended to pay the offender back for the crime. In the Bible this principle is described as 'an eye for an eye, and a tooth for a tooth'. A long custodial sentence is often seen by victims of crime as the best way to punish those who committed the crime against them.

The aim of deterrence

The punishment seeks to put the offender and others off (deter them from) committing crimes because they do not want to incur the punishment. A punishment for the aim of deterrence is a fine. 72 per cent of all offenders are fined.

The aim of reform

The punishment is devised to help the offender change so that he or she will no longer want to commit future criminal acts. It aims to show offenders that what they did was wrong. A punishment that seeks to reform the offender is a community punishment order.

The aim of vindication

Laws will only be respected if those breaking them are punished. The laws in a society must be respected if they are to work.

Test yourself

1 What is meant by a 'custodial sentence'?
2 What is meant by 'community service'?
3 (a) List the five aims of punishment.
(b) Give an example of three punishments to fit three of the five aims.

Punishment – what works?

Words you need to know

- **Parole** is the freeing of a prisoner before the end of their sentence because of good behaviour.

Does prison work?

Revision tip

It would be useful to know about an organisation that is working to reform the prison system and help offenders to reform. One example would be NACRO (The National Association for the Care and Resettlement of Offenders).

Prisons aim to reduce crime in three ways:

1 by deterring potential offenders

2 by protecting society by removing offenders from society

3 by encouraging prisoners to reform.

Imprisonment may meet the aim of retribution but it does not seem to deter people from committing crimes or to reform them. Over 58 per cent of those discharged from prison are reconvicted within two years. The prison population in England and Wales at the end of April 2001 was 65,800.

The reasons that prisons do not appear to be working include the following.

- The prison population has increased by 75 per cent over the last ten years. There are not enough warders to supervise activities so many offenders have to spend up to twenty-three hours a day in their cells.
- Many prisons are outdated and cells are overcrowded. There is evidence that this leads to stress and an increased risk of violence.
- Prisoners learn criminal behaviour from each other.
- Society has to be protected from offenders who are dangerous, but in fact, less than 50 per cent of the prisoners are guilty of violent crimes.
- Imprisonment breaks up families and many offenders have no support or home when they leave prison and so re-offend.
- Long-term sentences mean prisoners get institutionalised and find it difficult to cope with life outside prison.

Alternatives to prison

Research has highlighted that the chances of rehabilitation are greater the shorter the time an offender is in prison. Three recent initiatives introduced to seek to reduce the number of prisoners who re-offend by helping them to re-settle back into the community are:

- **The Home Detention Curfew (HDC)**: selected short-term prisoners spend up to the last two months of their prison sentence back at home. They have to be at home at night. If they break this curfew, they face being returned to prison. This system gets people back into the community.
- **Electronic tagging** is only allowed for offenders with prison sentences of less than four years, who are not thought to be a risk to the public, liable to try to escape, or to re-offend. The offender wears an electronic ankle tag and has to remain indoors for a set time each day, for example, overnight (as with HDC).
- The **parole system** is a way of trying to make prisoners understand where they are going wrong in life. The Parole Board assesses the offender's behaviour in prison and their risk of re-offending. If they think the prisoner has made good progress, they may release the prisoner from prison early. The person then has to remain in contact with the authorities for a set amount of time and their behaviour is monitored. Only around five per cent of those released from prison on parole re-offend during this set time.

The annual cost per prisoner in 2003 is £27,500. Organisations such as NACRO argue that there are better and cheaper ways of dealing with offenders. A community rehabilitation order costs on average £1,800 and a community punishment order £1,500. The cost of electronic tagging is about £4 per day. These sentences seem to have greater success in reducing the number of re-offenders and are cheaper.

Test yourself

1 How do prisons aim to reduce crime?
2 Give three arguments used to suggest that prisons do not reduce crime.
3 Outline the work of an organisation that seeks to help offenders and reform prisons.
4 (a) What is parole?
(b) Explain **two** other ways in which an offender may be released from prison early.
(c) Why do many people consider these punishments preferable to prison?

Capital punishment

Words you need to know *

- **Capital punishment** is punishment by death.

Capital punishment is the death penalty. There is no capital punishment in the UK, but it is still used in the USA and many other countries. It was a legal punishment in Britain up to 1965.

Capital punishment is seen as the ultimate means of **protecting** society from harm, of **retribution** for victims whose own life may have been taken, of **deterrence** for other criminals, and of **vindication** of the rule of law. However, many people oppose it because it obviously does not enable criminals to **reform**.

Arguments in favour of capital punishment

- The death penalty acts as a deterrent to murder. Since its abolition in this country, the number of murders and violent crimes has increased significantly.
- The death penalty removes the risk of the murderer repeating the crime. There have been murderers who have repeated their crime when freed from prison.
- The death penalty saves money, as society does not have to pay for the offender's upkeep in prison. The money could be used to help those in need.
- Some people regard the death sentence as more humane than a life sentence. There are murderers who have requested it (for example, Gary Gilmore in the USA requested that he be executed as he did not want to spend the rest of his life in prison).

Some Christians agree that capital punishment is a just form of punishment for these sorts of reasons. The Bible can be used to support this view – for example:

- **Genesis 9:6**: 'Whoever sheds the blood of a man, by man shall his blood be shed; for God made man in his own image.'
- **Leviticus 24:17**: 'He who kills a man shall be put to death.'
- The death penalty agrees with the right of revenge given by Moses: 'Show no pity: life for life, eye for an eye, a tooth for a tooth, hand for hand, foot for foot.' (**Deuteronomy 19:21**)

The Catholic Church does accept that capital punishment is an acceptable form of punishment when there is no other way to protect society. The Pope made a statement about this in **1995**.

Arguments against capital punishment

- A mistake could be made and an innocent person executed for a crime he or she did not commit. There is evidence that this has happened in the past.
- The death penalty punishes not only offenders but also their families because they lose a loved one.
- Capital punishment can create martyrs to a cause, for example, with terrorists.
- Execution is a barbaric and outdated practice in modern society.

Many Christians oppose capital punishment. Jesus taught that people should try to reform the offender, not seek revenge. Capital punishment removes any chance of reform.

- The sixth commandment orders people not to kill – life is sacred and only God should decide when it is to end.
- St Paul taught that revenge must be left to God. It is for God to seek vengeance not humans. Humans must seek to forgive and reform the offender.

Quakers (The Society of Friends) oppose capital punishment because of their belief that there is a 'spark of God' within everyone – human life is sacred.

In **1983** the General Synod of the Church of England debated capital punishment and agreed that it would 'deplore the reintroduction of capital punishment into the UK sentencing policy'. This was because it did not think capital punishment had any effect as a deterrent.

Revision tip

Knowing the details of the Catholic Church and Church of England teachings about the use of the death penalty will be useful for answering questions about capital punishment.

Test yourself

1 What is capital punishment?
2 When was capital punishment abolished in Britain?
3 Explain why some Christians are in favour of capital punishment.
4 Explain why some Christians are against capital punishment.

Christian attitudes to crime and punishment

Revision tip

Knowing the details of the Bible teachings below will be useful for answering questions about religious attitudes to crime and punishment from the Christian perspective.

Christian traditions agree that criminals should be punished by the state. But many Christians are concerned about the aims behind punishments. Most Christians require any punishment not to seek to take revenge on the offender but seek to help the individual to reform. Forgiveness is also a very important part of Christian teaching.

Christians look at the teaching of Jesus and St Paul as a guide to how offenders should be punished.

The woman caught in adultery

In the incident of the woman caught in adultery (**John 8:2–11**), Jesus does not deny the Jewish law that the punishment for adultery is death by stoning. He merely says that anyone free from sin may throw the first stone. Only God was considered to be perfect, therefore no one dared to throw a stone, as they would have been guilty of blasphemy. Jesus was left alone with the woman. He refused to condemn her and told her to reform. Christians believe that this incident is teaching that they must seek to forgive and help offenders to reform.

The incident of the penitent thief

Jesus was crucified between two thieves. In the incident of the penitent thief (**Luke 23:32–43**), one of the thieves is sorry (penitent) for what he has done. He recognises Jesus as the Messiah and asks that Jesus remember him. Jesus answers that he will enter heaven with him. The man is dying but God can still forgive him. The incident would suggest that it is never too late to turn to God. The criminal recognises Jesus' power to save him from the punishment he deserves for his sins. By turning to Jesus he is able to gain forgiveness.

Jesus used parables to teach his followers his message about forgiveness. Two of Jesus' parables, the Parable of the Lost Son and the Parable of the Unmerciful Servant, teach about forgiveness and may be applied to Christian attitudes to punishing offenders.

The lost son

The Parable of the Lost Son (**Luke 15:11–32**) is about two sons. The younger son goes away from home and spends his inheritance while his brother remains at home and continues to work on the farm. When the younger son's money runs out, he returns home and is welcomed back by his father. His older brother will not welcome him home. The older son thought he deserved a reward as he has always done as his father wished. By not welcoming his brother home, he showed that he was not the loyal son he believed himself to be. The father represents God and the sons represent ordinary people. The teaching is that God is willing to forgive sinners who are sorry and turn to him and therefore people should be willing to do the same.

The unmerciful servant

In the Parable of the Unmerciful Servant (**Matthew 18:23–35**), a servant owed his master a large sum of money. The master was willing to cancel the debt when the servant asked. A fellow servant owed the same servant a smaller sum. The amount was equal to only a day's wages, but the servant would not show his fellow servant the same compassion his master had shown him. His master was angry and had him severely punished. The usual understanding of this parable by Christians is that the master (God) is willing to welcome back sinners if they turn to him. People must show God that they are sorry for their sins. If God can forgive so much then people must show the same willingness to forgive others.

In conclusion, most people believe that God will forgive the sins of people who are sorry and turn to him. They believe that they must offer forgiveness to offenders and help them to reform. Society must protect the innocent and punish crimes. Some Christians say that you should hate the sin but love the sinner. Many Christians believe punishments must, in the end, help people to reform and become the person God intended that person to be.

Test yourself

1. What does the story of the woman caught in adultery teach Christians about the use of punishment?
2. (a) Why is the son described as 'lost' in the parable?
   (b) What is this parable teaching about forgiveness and reconciliation?
3. What does the Parable of the Unmerciful Servant teach about forgiveness?
4. Why might a Christian object to a punishment that does not encourage reform?

The rich in society

Words you need to know

- **Inherited wealth** is money that is passed on from one generation of a family to another.
- **'Fat cat' salaries** are huge sums of money paid as wages or bonuses to top executives.
- The **National Lottery** is a betting system that raises money for good causes.
- **Indolence** is laziness and the wish to avoid activity or exertion.

Bill Gates is estimated to have a personal fortune of £53 billion

The ways in which people have become millionaires in Britain include:

- **Inheriting wealth** from the estate of someone who has died, usually a relative. Some families have enormous wealth and pass this on to the next generation.
- Being paid a **'fat cat' salary**. This is a term used to describe the salaries of top company executives. The annual salaries and bonuses of these executives may be over £1 million.
- They have had six winning numbers in the **National Lottery** draw and become millionaires.
- They have invented or manufactured something that has sold very well. For example, Bill Gates developed software for personal computers that has made his company very successful and him very rich.

Christian attitudes to wealth

Jesus never said that it was wrong to be rich, only that wealth must not blind people to the needs of others and how God wants them to behave. People who are rich have a duty to share what they have with those who are poor.

In the Sermon on the Mount (**Matthew 6:19–24**), Jesus warned of the dangers of wealth. Jesus warned people not to 'store up for yourselves treasures on earth, where moth and rust destroy, and where thieves break in and steal'. People should put their efforts into storing up 'treasures in heaven' because these will not decay or be stolen. 'Treasures in heaven' means actions God approves of such as helping people in need. Jesus said that people cannot 'serve two masters' – people cannot serve both God and money.

On another occasion, Jesus said that it was 'easier for a camel to go through the eye of a needle than for a rich man to enter the kingdom of God' (**Matthew 19:24–30**). Jesus meant that sometimes riches can 'blind' people to the real priorities of life. He said that people must be willing to give up their possessions to follow God, but this is difficult for many rich people as their wealth means so much to them.

An example of how difficult it might be for some people to give up their wealth occurred in the incident of the rich young man (**Mark 10:17–22**). The rich young man asked Jesus what he must do 'to inherit eternal life?' Jesus told him to keep God's commandments, to sell everything and to give the money to the poor. Then, having given up his wealth, he was to follow Jesus. The young man was unable to part with his wealth.

Many rich people have put this teaching to help the less fortunate into practise. They have established foundations so that some of their wealth is used for good causes. This follows the example of the early church who by 'selling their possessions and goods, they gave to anyone as he had need' (**Acts 2:45**).

An example of such work is the Bill and Melinda Gates Foundation, which is dedicated to improving people's lives by sharing advances in health and learning with the global community.

Revision tip

Knowing the details of Jesus' teachings on wealth will be useful for answering questions about religious attitudes to rich and poor in society.

What is your example ... ?

It will be useful in your exam to know some details about an individual or organisation that has used wealth to help less fortunate people, like the Bill and Melinda Gates Foundation, for example. What is your example?

Test yourself

1 State and explain **three** ways in which people may become wealthy.
2 Why might Christians believe that they must use some of their wealth for the good of others? Refer to religious teaching in your answer.
3 Describe how some of the wealthy people of the world seek to use some of their wealth to help those who are poor.

The poor in society

Words you need to know

- **Minimum wage**: the lowest wage that can legally be paid for most types of work.

There are many people in Britain who live below the poverty line. This means that they have barely enough to live on. Poor people often live in areas of high crime and bad housing. The government provides people who are unemployed or do not earn very much with financial support through social security benefits.

Social security is a term used for financial help for those who need it, in whatever form it may take. In Britain the reasons why financial assistance are given include:

- the relief of poverty
- social protection, not just against poverty from unemployment or low earnings, but against hardships if people become sick, to help families with child care, and so on
- redistribution of wealth so that the rich provide some support for the poor. Social security is not charity, but a just way of running a society.

The minimum wage

Another way the government seeks to help the poor is the minimum wage. This is aimed at providing employees with decent minimum standards and fairness in the workplace. It applies to nearly all workers and sets hourly rates below which pay must not be allowed to fall. For example, in 2002 the adult rate for workers aged twenty-two and over was £4.20 per hour and the rate for workers aged eighteen to twenty-one was £3.60 per hour.

Unemployment

Unemployment exists when someone cannot get a job. Unemployment is one of the major causes of poverty in Britain because people do not earn a wage or start a career that will pay them more as they develop their skills.

Causes of unemployment

- Firms closing because they no longer make enough money.

- New technology means that a smaller workforce is needed.
- The country's or the world's economy slumps and there is less money to create new jobs.
- People's skills become outdated and no longer in demand.
- Companies employ people for short periods only, rather than permanently.

Homelessness

Many people end up sleeping on the streets, in bed-and-breakfast accommodation or hostels because they cannot afford to buy or rent a place of their own. People without a home find it difficult to get a job, social security, or to rent a house because they have no permanent address at which they can be contacted. It is a vicious circle of poverty.

There are many reasons why people may become homeless

There are many reasons why people become homeless, including:

- children running away from home because of problems at home or at school
- addiction to drugs or alcohol that leads to loss of job, family breakdown, and so on
- addiction to gambling so that rental or mortgage payments are not kept up
- marriage break ups.

Homeless people have a right to be housed by their local authority, who will pay for bed-and-breakfast accommodation. There are also lists for housing, which homeless people can join.

Test yourself

1 (a) What is unemployment?
  (b) Explain **three** causes of unemployment.

2 (a) What is homelessness?
  (b) Explain **three** causes of homelessness.

Caring for the poor

Two hundred years ago many people thought that the rich deserved to be rich because they worked hard. The poor, it was thought, could stop being poor if they worked hard, stayed away from drink and gambling, and behaved decently and respectfully.

Today, some people still hold this kind of view. Other people, however, think that society has a responsibility to help those who are living in poverty.

Religious traditions today are all very involved in helping combat poverty, whether in this country or abroad. Religious organisations often have a very important role in local communities, organising food for the homeless, and services and support for the unemployed and those below the poverty line. This is because religious traditions believe that God wishes people to help those worse off than them.

In the Christian tradition, for example, Jesus' teachings about the poor are central to how Christians believe God wishes them to live. Jesus said that the poor were just as important as the rich and had special favour with God. In the Sermon on the Mount, Jesus said: 'Blessed are you who are poor, for yours is the kingdom of heaven' (**Luke 6:20–21**).

Jesus taught that everyone should take responsibility for caring for the poor. Jesus' cousin, John the Baptist, shared his belief and said that a person who had two coats should share with someone who had none and a person who had food should share it with someone who had none (**Luke 3:10–12**).

Christians today try to follow this teaching in different ways: through giving to charity, by helping out in community centres and hostels, and through supporting the work of organisations that help the poor.

Revision tip

You need to be able to refer to **two** religious traditions in answers about religious attitudes to rich and poor in society.

What is your example … ?

It may be useful to know an example of a religious organisation that works to combat poverty. There are two examples here from two different religious traditions: the Salvation Army and the Catholic Church. You may have a different example or examples of your own to revise.

The Salvation Army is a Christian tradition with a long history of working with the poor. The Salvation Army is a Protestant denomination that was founded in 1878 by William and Catherine Booth. One of the areas the Salvation Army works in today is to collect money and run shelters for homeless people. Around the world, 38,000 people are given shelter throughout the year in more than 800 hostels.

William Booth

Another example of an organisation that works to combat poverty is CAFOD. CAFOD stands for the 'Catholic Fund for Overseas Development'. CAFOD members raise money from Catholics and others in this country to fund many different programmes. It works to provide short-term relief in emergencies like earthquakes or floods. It has long-term programmes of helping poor people to find a way out of poverty. CAFOD also does a lot of research into poverty – what causes it and how best to help poor people around the world. It also campaigns to put pressure on governments to be fairer towards the poor.

Test yourself

1 Describe religious teachings for **one** religious tradition about caring for the poor.
2 Give examples of how religious believers try to help the poor.
3 Describe the work of **two** organisations with a religious background that work to combat poverty.

The National Lottery

Many people hope to become rich by winning the National Lottery

The National Lottery has given many people hope that they could become extremely rich. Many people are concerned that the lottery has encouraged more people to gamble and there is the risk of addiction to gambling. As a result, people get into debt to pay for their habit. There is also concern that some people spend money they cannot afford on lottery tickets in the hope of getting rich.

The aim of the National Lottery is to support good causes. Twenty-eight pence of ever £1 spent on a lottery ticket goes to good causes in Britain. The money raised includes support for:

- the arts
- sport
- National Heritage – historic buildings, cultural events, and so on
- charities.

Christian attitudes to the lottery

Some Christians believe that the damage that the National Lottery could do to society by encouraging gambling outweighs the advantages of the money raised for good causes. These Christians argue that Jesus taught people to put their trust in God and not worry about their income.

In the Sermon on the Mount (**Matthew 6:25–33**), Jesus told people not to worry about whether they have food or clothes, as God will care for them. Jesus taught that it is more important to try to live a life that follows God's laws.

St Paul warned his friend Timothy (**1 Timothy 6:9–10**) that the love of money is at the root of evil. St Paul said that:

> *people who want to get rich fall into temptation and a trap and into many foolish and harmful desires that plunge men into ruin and destruction. For the love of money is a root of all kinds of evil. Some people, eager for money, have wandered from the faith and pierced themselves with many griefs.*

Most Christians would prefer to work for charities that seek to help the poor rather than to encourage people to buy lottery tickets. There are a number of Christian organisations that exist to tackle poverty (see the examples on pages 59).

What is your example ... ?

It will be useful in your exam to know some details about an individual or organisation that seeks to help people addicted to gambling. Our example is Gamblers Anonymous. What is your example?

Gamblers Anonymous

Gamblers Anonymous is a fellowship of men and women who have joined together to do something about their own gambling problem and to help other compulsive gamblers to do the same. Gamblers Anonymous sees compulsive gambling as an illness that can never be cured but can be controlled by following a very simple programme. The reasons that the organisation lists for people becoming compulsive gamblers includes:

- inability and unwillingness to accept reality, which results in people spending a lot of time creating images of what they will do when they make the 'big win'
- emotional insecurity: the compulsive gambler only finds emotional security when gambling
- immaturity: the desire to have all good things in life without any great effort is a common character pattern of the problem gambler.

Compulsive gamblers apply a twelve-step recovery plan in their lives. These steps are basically spiritual in their concept. The first stage involves admitting that he or she is powerless over gambling and that their lives have become unmanageable. They accept that a power greater than themselves could restore a normal way of thinking and living. They humbly ask 'God (of our understanding)' to remove their shortcomings and that through prayer and meditation to improve their conscious contact with 'God (as we understand Him)'; praying only for knowledge of His will and the power to carry that out.

Test yourself

1 What is the National Lottery?
2 Why are some religious believers concerned about the National Lottery?
3 Why might other religious believers think that the National Lottery is a good idea?
4 (a) Outline the work of an organisation that seeks to help compulsive gamblers.
  (b) Why might a religious believer support the work of this organisation?
5 'The love of money is a source of all kinds of evil.' Do you agree with this statement? Give reasons for your answer.

Practice essay questions

There are two types of question in your exam: a stimulus response question and a structured essay question. A stimulus response question is when you get some kind of information, like a table or a picture, for example, and then some short questions about it. There will be one compulsory stimulus response question in your exam. This will be on Section A of your course – 'Truth and spirituality,' (Unit 1 in this book). In Section B of your exam, you will have six structured essay questions to choose from. You have to do three of these. The questions will always be based on the six topics covered in Units 2–7 of this book: 'Matters of life', 'Matters of death', 'Drug abuse', 'Media and technology', 'Crime and punishment' and 'Rich and poor in society'.

This section of the book gives you some structured essays to practise. They are not actual exam questions but questions that will help you practise structuring your answer. At the end of each section are notes for each question. You can check your answer against these – they are for guidance only because you might look at different examples or different arguments. They are also written out as points to check your answer against, not as structured essay questions. **Do not answer structured essay questions as a list or a list of bullet points!**

If you are going to revise successfully, attempt each essay question before you look at the guidance notes for each question.

If there are points you have missed then go back and look at the relevant revision section in the book and your class notes.

Section A: The nature of truth and spirituality

In your exam, you will have a stimulus response question for this section. You will not be writing a structured essay question on the nature of truth and spirituality. To revise for this section, make sure you know the topic well – make sure you are clear on the meaning of the special words used in this topic, like 'conscience' and 'abstract reasoning', and on the different arguments used. The 'Test yourself' questions in Unit 1 of this book will help you revise these. Your teacher will be able to give you examples of stimulus response questions to practise.

Section B: Religious responses to contemporary issues

(These questions are on topics covered in Units 2, 3, 4, 5, 6 and 7 of this study guide.)

In this section of the exam, you will choose **three** questions out of a list of six. Each question will be broken down into different parts. These will be structured essay questions.

The questions here are sample essay questions for you to practise. There are some tips on answering them on pages 66–79.

Sample question 1

B2 Matters of life

(a) Explain what is meant by artificial insemination and why it is used. (*5 marks*)

(b) Describe what is meant by cloning and explain how people's religious beliefs will affect their attitude to cloning. (*10 marks*)

(c) 'Research using human embryos is acceptable.' Do you agree? Give reasons for your answer, showing that you have thought about more than one point of view. Refer to religious teachings in your answer. (*5 marks*)

Sample question 2

B3 Matters of death

(a) What is a hospice? Why do many religious believers support the work of hospices? (*5 marks*)

(b) Explain religious attitudes towards euthanasia. (*10 marks*)

(c) 'It's my life so I should have the right to decide when to end it.' Do you agree? Give reasons for your answer, showing that you have thought about more than one point of view. Refer to religious teachings in your answer. (*5 marks*)

Sample question 3

B4 Drug abuse

(a) Explain what is meant by the term 'performance enhancing drugs'. (*5 marks*)

(b) How might religious teachings and beliefs influence a person's view on drinking alcohol and smoking tobacco? (*10 marks*)

(c) 'If I want to take cannabis then I should be allowed to.' Do you agree? Give reasons for your answer, showing that you have thought about more than one point of view. Refer to religious teachings in your answer. (*5 marks*)

Sample question 4

B5 Media and technology

(a) Explain what is meant by the term 'the media'. (*5 marks*)

(b) Explain the concerns that a religious person might have about the influence of television and films on society. (*10 marks*)

(c) 'Religious people should not try to stop me watching what I want.' Do you agree? Give reasons for your answer, showing that you have thought about more than one point of view. Refer to religious teachings in your answer. (*5 marks*)

Sample question 5

B6 Crime and punishment

(a) State and explain **four** aims of punishment. (*5 marks*)

(b) Why might a religious person work for an organisation that helps with the care and resettlement of offenders? (*10 marks*)

(c) 'Capital punishment in Britain should never be brought back.' Do you agree? Give reasons for your answer, showing that you have thought about more than one point of view. Refer to religious teachings in your answer. (*5 marks*)

Sample question 6

B7 Rich and poor in society

(a) Why might a religious person be concerned about the effect of great wealth on a person? (*5 marks*)

(b) Explain religious attitudes towards wealth and possessions. (*10 marks*)

(c) 'Everyone should buy lottery tickets to help good causes.' Do you agree? Give reasons for your answer, showing that you have thought about more than one point of view. Refer to religious teachings in your answer. (*5 marks*)

Guidance notes

These notes are to give you some guidance on your answers to the practice essay questions on pages 63–65. You may have used different examples or looked at different religious traditions in your answers, which is fine – these notes just suggest some possible answers. Also, these guidance notes are just notes – remember to answer structured essay questions as proper essays. **Do not answer structured essay questions as a list or a list of bullet points!**

Section B: Religious responses to contemporary issues

Sample question 1

(a) Explain what is meant by artificial insemination and why it is used.

Artificial insemination involves injecting sperm from the male partner into the female partner's reproductive tract. For most couples, it is performed with the husband's sperm. However, when the husband's sperm contains few or no live sperm, the couple may consider using donor sperm insemination.

Artificial insemination is used when the couple have had problems conceiving a child and it is found that the woman has a problem in conceiving.

(b) Describe what is meant by cloning and explain how people's religious beliefs will affect their attitude to cloning.

Cloning is an aspect of genetic engineering that allows for the reproduction of identical creatures.

Which religious tradition or traditions you use here is up to you. These notes refer to Christian traditions.

Most Christians are not against animal cloning so long as the animals are cared for and treated with respect. This is because the cloning of animals could help to solve the problems of hunger in the developing world. The Parable of the Sheep and the Goats warns Christians that they may be judged on how they have helped hungry people and therefore cloning is one way that this might be done.

Many Christians are against the cloning of humans. This is because they believe that each person is the unique creation of God and has a special relationship with God. Psalm 138:13–16 states that God created every part of a person and knew that person before they were born. For many Christians, cloning goes against the sanctity of life, as they believe it is not showing sufficient respect for human life.

Even Christians who support the practice of cloning believe that scientists must be carefully controlled so that they do not try to create a 'super-race'. Christians believe that in God's eyes everyone is equal and such a creation would go against this belief. It would also disrupt the natural order planned by God. If scientists do not take care then there is the risk of permanent damage to the human genome that cannot be undone. Again, this would destroy the human race as created by God.

(c) 'Research using human embryos is acceptable.' Do you agree? Give reasons for your answer, showing that you have thought about more than one point of view. Refer to religious teachings in your answer.

These guidance notes consider Christian traditions. You may have used different religious traditions or examples in your answer.

Arguments **for** *the statement might include:*

- *The teaching of Jesus made it clear that the sick must be helped. Therefore, embryo research is one way in which congenital diseases and chromosome abnormalities may be cured.*
- *When it states in Genesis that God made us in 'his image', it means that God has given us the ability to learn and develop. Genetic engineering may be part of God's plan for human development and the solving of many problems that limit humans' quality of life.*
- *The Church of England is against the production of embryos specifically for research and does not believe any embryos should be used after they are fourteen days old. However, before the fourteenth day, the Church of England does not believe life has begun and therefore it is acceptable to use spare embryos from fertility treatment for research.*
- *The Methodist Church supports genetic engineering if it is used to improve the health of the world, but not if it is used to exploit anyone.*

Reasons **against** *the statement might include:*

- *Some Christians believe that the work of the genetic engineers might be going against God's plan for the world and fear that scientists are seeking to put themselves in the place of God.*
- *The Catholic Church believes life begins at the moment of conception and therefore embryos are human beings made in the image of God and possessing a soul. The Catholic Church teaches that embryology is a sin.*

In your **conclusion** *you need to weigh up the evidence for and against the statement and decide whether or not you think embryology is right. You are making a judgment based on the evidence you have presented in your answer and coming to a conclusion. Support your conclusion with religious teaching. For example, you may share the Quaker view that the matter needs to be considered very carefully as it could lead to future problems for the human race, of which we are currently unaware.*

Sample question 2

(a) What is a hospice? Why do many religious believers support the work of hospices?

This sample answer looks at Christian believers: you might have chosen a different religious tradition.

A hospice is a type of hospital that is concerned with the care of terminally ill patients. A hospice seeks to not only care for the physical welfare of the patient but also his or her spiritual needs. There will be counsellors available for people to discuss their fears about dying. Their family and friends also receive support to help them to cope with the situation. Most hospices have Christian origins, but hospice care is available to all regardless of their religious beliefs.

Jesus helped anyone in need and Christians believe that they should do the same. In the Parable of the Sheep and the Goats, Jesus warned people that they would be judged on how they had helped the sick and many Christians believe that working in a hospice is one way in which they can do this. The Parable of the Good Samaritan teaches that everyone is our neighbour and is to be helped.

Jesus helped the sick and dying and Christians believe that supporting the work of hospices is following his example. Jesus always showed compassion and the terminally ill and their families need such compassion.

(b) Explain religious attitudes towards euthanasia.

- *Human life is sacred and given by God. Religious believers have to consider very carefully when life ends and what rights they have to end a life.*
- *Look at the reasons for and against euthanasia in your answer.*
- *You need to include religious attitudes of different religious traditions. You could consider the different attitudes of Christians to the use of passive and active euthanasia on pages 24.*

(c) 'It's my life so I should have the right to decide when to end it.' Do you agree? Give reasons for your answer, showing that you have thought about more than one point of view. Refer to religious teachings in your answer.

These guidance notes consider Christian traditions. You may have used different religious traditions or examples in your answer.

Reasons in **favour** *of the statement could include:*

- *Christians believe that we were made in the image of God and this means that God has given us the freedom to make our own decisions. This includes the right to end our own lives.*

- *If a person is no longer aware of their identity then they could be considered dead. It is only the physical body that remains and people should be allowed to leave a living will to ensure that they will not be resuscitated if they have lost their sense of identity.*
- *Modern advances in medicine often extend life when the person is not really alive at all. This may be going against God's plan and the person should be allowed to die with dignity.*

Reasons **against** *the statement could include:*

- *Life is a gift from God and is sacred. It is not for us to end it.*
- *Suffering is a test of faith (as seen in the Bible story of Job) and so it must be endured. Euthanasia and suicide is showing a lack of trust in God and is a sin.*
- *God has decided the length of each individual life and so it is wrong to shorten the God-given time span.*

In your **conclusion** *you need to weigh up the evidence for and against the statement and decide whether or not you think it is right for a person to decide to end his or her life. You are making a judgment based on the evidence you have presented in your answer and coming to a conclusion. Support your conclusion with religious teaching. For example, you may share the Quaker view that those who consider taking their own life need support and compassion, not condemnation. You might also refer to the work of the Samaritans.*

Sample question 3

(a) Explain what is meant by the term 'performance enhancing drugs.'

Performance enhancing drugs are drugs, such as anabolic steroids, taken by sports people to improve sporting performance, which enable people to train harder and build muscle more quickly.

(b) How might religious teachings and beliefs influence a person's view on drinking alcohol and smoking tobacco?

These guidance notes look at examples from the Christian traditions. You may have looked at other religious traditions in your answer.

You need to include reference to the attitudes of different religious traditions in your answer to this question. Christians have different views on whether or not alcohol and smoking damages 'the body as a temple of the Holy Spirit'. Christians are also concerned about the links between crime and alcohol.

There are many Christians such as Quakers who advocate total abstinence from smoking and drinking alcohol because of the harm it does to the individual and others. St Paul taught that people should not do anything that could be harmful to others. Passive smoking is a cause of cancer and many crimes are committed under the influence of alcohol.

The Salvation Army does not allow its officers to smoke. Every Salvationist makes a commitment to live an alcohol-free life. The Salvation Army is also concerned of the effect of alcohol, not only on people's health but also as a cause of many of the crimes in society. Many members of the Salvation Army work with alcoholics to help them to overcome their addiction.

Many Free Churches such as the Baptists use non-alcoholic wine during the services of Holy Communion because alcohol is seen as a cause of many of the evils of modern society. These Christian traditions do not want to encourage the use of alcohol.

Most Catholics and members of the Church of England (Anglicans) would argue that alcohol, if taken in moderation, is acceptable.

- *They use alcoholic wine during their services of Holy Communion because Jesus used alcoholic wine and it provides a direct link with the event.*
- *Catholics and Anglicans believe that as Jesus and St Paul drank wine then they can do the same.*
- *Jesus' first miracle was to turn water into wine during the celebration of the marriage at Cana.*

- *Jesus gave the Apostles wine to represent his blood at the Last Supper.*
- *St Paul did not say that people were to give up the drinking of alcohol, only to use it in moderation. St Paul advised his friend Timothy in a letter to 'stop drinking only water, and use a little wine because of your stomach and your frequent illnesses'.*

(c) 'If I want to take cannabis then I should be allowed to.' Do you agree? Give reasons for your answer, showing that you have thought about more than one point of view. Refer to religious teachings in your answer.

Reasons **for** *the statement could include:*

- *God has given people free will and it is up to each individual to decide what to do with his or her body.*
- *Cannabis is not addictive and is less harmful than alcohol.*
- *Few crimes are committed because people have taken cannabis.*
- *It can be helpful to relieve the suffering of people with illnesses such as multiple sclerosis. From the Christian perspective, Jesus helped the sick and if cannabis is a way of relieving suffering then people should be allowed to use it.*

Reasons **against** *the statement could include:*

- *People have rights but they must not be allowed to take an action that could be harmful to others. A driver under the influence of cannabis is a danger on the road and, as cannabis stays in the body longer than alcohol, the driver may not be aware of the dangers.*
- *People say that they need to take cannabis to relieve stress, but many Christians, for example, would argue that if they put their trust in God there is no need to take drugs. Jesus said that if people trust in God they do not need to 'worry about tomorrow, for tomorrow will worry about itself. Each day has enough trouble of its own'.*
- *Cannabis can lead people to take 'hard' drugs and there is a greater risk of the crimes associated with such drugs.*
- *The long-term effects of taking cannabis could be harmful and are not as yet known. Many religious believers would argue that we must not take any actions that may harm the bodies that God has given us.*
- *Cannabis may not be addictive, but there is evidence that people become psychologically dependent on cannabis.*

In your **conclusion** *you need to weigh up the evidence for and against the statement and decide whether or not you think it is right for cannabis to be legalised. You are making a* *judgment based on the evidence you have presented in your answer and coming to a conclusion. Support your conclusion with religious teaching. For example, you may share the view of many Christians that people should not do anything that can result in other people being harmed. St Paul said that 'it is better not to eat meat or drink wine or to do anything else that will cause your brother to fall'.*

Sample question 4

(a) Explain what is meant by the term 'the media'.

You need to explain that the media is the main means of mass communication in the world today and include examples such as newspapers, music, television, cinema, the Internet, and satellite communications.

(b) Explain the concerns that a religious person might have about the influence of television and films on society.

These guidance notes look at attitudes from the Christian traditions. You may have used different religious traditions in your answer.

Many Christians are concerned that children watch television and videos or access the Internet unsupervised by adults. There is concern that the watching of unsuitable programmes or playing unsuitable games has led to an increase in anti-social behaviour. It is argued that the increased use of bad language and violence in society is the result of media influences.

Most Christians believe that they have a duty to ensure that children are protected. St Paul taught that people must 'flee from sexual immorality' because the 'body is a temple of the Holy Spirit' and to use it to honour God. Many Christians believe that by encouraging people to behave in an anti-social way is to go against this instruction.

Christians believe that Jesus taught people in the Sermon on the Mount not to be worried about possessions. The important thing is to build up 'treasures in heaven', that is, living a life as God would wish. Yet advertising in the media has led people into debt because they purchase products that they cannot afford. Advertising encourages people to think that material possessions are the most important thing in life. Christians believe that the most important influence on people's lives should be working for God.

Many Christians are concerned that the influence of role models in the media is not always a good one. For example, the media's emphasis on body image is thought to be one of the causes of the increase in the number of people with eating disorders such as anorexia and bulimia. Christians believe that God created them and God loves each person. Most Christians believe that what matters to God are not the way we look but the way we behave.

St Paul taught that in a Christian society, 'there must not be even a hint of sexual immorality' and yet many Christians believe that the emphasis of the media is on sexual matters. St Paul also instructed that there should not 'be obscenity, foolish talk or coarse joking', but many Christians feel that many television programmes and films contain inappropriate material. There is concern that the increase in sex-related crimes might be the result of the emphasis on sex in the media.

(c) 'Religious people should not try to stop me watching what I want.' Do you agree? Give reasons for your answer, showing that you have thought about more than one point of view. Refer to religious teachings in your answer.

These guidance notes look at attitudes from the Christian traditions. You may have used different religious traditions in your answer.

Reasons **for** *the statement might include:*

- *As only eleven per cent of the population attend a place of Christian worship regularly then it is not right for the minority to seek to impose their views on the majority.*
- *People are capable of distinguishing between fact and fiction and capable of making their own decisions of what is appropriate to watch. Just because people see violence in television dramas, it does not mean that they are going to go out and copy it. If there is anti-social behaviour in society, there are probably other causes rather than media influences.*
- *The British Film Board and the TV watershed give guidance of what will be inappropriate viewing for children. Parents should make the decisions about what access they give their children to the media, not religious believers.*

Reasons **against** *the statement might include:*

- *Most Christians believe that the very fact that they are Christians means that they must spread the Christian message. They would feel that they have a duty to speak out against things that are wrong in society. For example, if Christians such as Martin Luther King had not tried to stop racial discrimination in the USA then black people might still not have civil rights. The spreading of Martin Luther King's message around the world by the media gave support to the cause that forced the USA to give black people civil rights.*
- *The work of Christians such as Mary Whitehouse led to the introduction of the TV watershed and if it were not for such people monitoring the media then the bad influences of the media might outweigh the good.*
- *The cultural tradition of the country is Christian and there should be some coverage of religious and spiritual matters, especially at Christmas and Easter.*
- *In your* **conclusion** *you need to weigh up the evidence for and against the statement and decide whether or not you think it is right for one group to impose their views on another. You are making a judgment based on the evidence you have presented in your answer and coming to a conclusion. Support your conclusion with religious teaching. For example, you may share the view of many Christians that people should not do anything that can result in other people being harmed. St Paul said that 'it is better not to eat meat or drink wine or to do anything else that will cause your brother to fall'.*

Sample question 5

(a) State and explain four aims of punishment.

Four aims of punishment are protection, retribution, deterrence and reformation. (You could also have chosen vindication. Vindication is the view that if laws are to be respected, there must be punishment when they are broken.)

- *The aim of protection is to protect society from anti-social behaviour by stopping offenders repeating their actions. A punishment that could be given with the aim of protection is a driving ban for dangerous driving.*
- *The aim of retribution is to pay the offender back for the crime. A punishment with the aim of retribution is imprisonment.*
- *The aim of deterrence seeks to put the offender and others off committing crimes because they do not want to incur the punishment. A punishment for the aim of deterrence is a fine.*
- *The aim of reform is devised to help the offender change so that he or she will no longer want to commit future criminal acts. It aims to show offenders that what they did is wrong. A punishment that seeks to reform the offender is a community punishment order.*

(b) Why might a religious person work for an organisation that helps with the care and resettlement of offenders?

These guidance notes look at attitudes from the Christian traditions. You may have used different religious traditions in your answer.

St Paul taught that the authority of the State must be obeyed and most Christians accept that offenders must be punished. However, they believe that the teaching of Jesus makes it clear that although they may dislike what the offender did, a Christian still has a duty to help them.

In the Parable of the Sheep and the Goats, prison visiting is mentioned as being a good deed. Jesus forgave the woman caught in adultery and the penitent thief. One way in which Christians today could follow Jesus' example and show forgiveness is to help offenders to find a job or home when they leave prison, or be a prison visitor.

In the Parables of the Lost Son and the Unmerciful Servant, Jesus repeated his teaching that as God is willing to forgive those who are sorry for their actions then Christians must do the same. By seeking to reform prisoners and to seek to find punishments that will help the offender to reform, Christians might feel that they are demonstrating this willingness to 'love their neighbour' even if that neighbour has broken the law.

It would be a very good idea to include an example of an organisation that helps with the care and resettlement of offenders in your answer. One example could be NACRO, The National Association for the Care and Resettlement of Offenders.

(c) 'Capital punishment in Britain should never be brought back.' Do you agree? Give reasons for your answer, showing that you have thought about more than one point of view. Refer to religious teachings in your answer.

Reasons **for** *the statement include:*

- *From a Christian perspective, compare your answer with the points on page 50 of this study guide. You must make sure that you include religious teaching in your answer.*

Reasons **against** *the statement include:*

- *From a Christian perspective, compare your answer with the points on pages 51 of this study guide. You must make sure that you include religious teaching in your answer.*

In your **conclusion** *you need to weigh up the evidence for and against the statement and explain that capital punishment is an issue over which religious believers are divided. If you are looking at the Christian traditions, you could explain that the major reason Christians are divided is that biblical teaching can be used to support both points of view, especially Moses' teaching of 'a life for life, eye for an eye, a tooth for a tooth, hand for hand, foot for foot' (Deuteronomy 19:21). Some Christians interpret the passage to mean that a life must be taken for a life, whereas other Christians understand the instruction to mean the murderer should pay the family of the victim money equal to the value of the life taken.*

Sample question 6

(a) Why might a religious person be concerned about the effect of great wealth on a person?

Christians might be concerned that the person could become indolent and not do anything useful for society. Out of boredom, the effect of the great wealth might be to make the person turn to alcohol or drugs and Christians might be concerned of the effect on their body as a 'temple to the Holy Spirit'. The wealth might blind them to the needs of others and the love of their wealth might cause them to forget what God requires of them.

(b) Explain religious attitudes towards wealth and possessions.

These guidance notes look at the attitudes of Christian traditions. You may have used different religious traditions in your answer.

Christians recognise that wealth and possessions do not always bring happiness. The main theme of Christian teaching is that wealth must not blind a person to the needs of others.

- *The rich young man wanted to know how to get into heaven, but when told to give up his wealth was unable to do so and, as Jesus pointed out, it is easier for a camel to 'go through the eye of a needle than for a rich man to enter heaven', meaning that wealth can 'blind' people to the real priorities of life.*
- *Christians should be storing up 'treasures in heaven' that will be valued by God and not possessions in this world, as wealth and possessions do not last.*
- *Christians recognise that God wishes they should help those in need by supporting charity work.*

(c) 'Everyone should buy lottery tickets to help good causes.' Do you agree? Give reasons for your answer, showing that you have thought about more than one point of view. Refer to religious teachings in your answer.

Reasons **for** *the statement might include:*

- *Twenty-eight pence from every £1 spent on lottery tickets goes to support good causes including charities, therefore it helps people in need.*
- *Simply collecting for charity would not raise the amount of money that the lottery does. It is only by thinking that they will get a big win that people are willing to buy lottery tickets.*
- *The lottery is not really betting on anything so it is not likely to encourage people to gamble.*

Reasons **against** *the statement might include:*

- *The desire to get rich through a lottery win is encouraging people to buy more lottery tickets than they can afford.*
- *The National Lottery encourages gambling and religious believers should not be involved in any activity that can lead to addictions and debt.*
- *Most religious believers feel that they should put their trust in God and not be concerned in trying to get rich. For example, Jesus taught in the Sermon on the Mount that people should not worry about possessions because God will care for them as he does all of nature.*

In your **conclusion** *you need to weigh up the evidence for and against the statement and decide whether or not you agree with the question. You are making a judgment based on the evidence you have presented in your answer and coming to a conclusion. Support your conclusion with religious teaching. For example, you may share the view of many Christians that people should not do anything that may result in other people being harmed. St Paul said that 'It is better not to eat meat or drink wine or do anything else that will cause your borther to fall'.*